MORE
GOOD
CLEAN
JOKES

Bob Phillips

HARVEST HOUSE PUBLISHERS
Irvine, California 92707

MORE GOOD CLEAN JOKES

DEDICATED TO

EVERYONE WHO BUYS MY

SECOND JOKE BOOK

INTRODUCTION

After the publication of my first joke book, *The World's Greatest Collection of Clean Jokes*, I had many requests but I decided to ignore them all and write another joke book anyway.

You see, a joke book writer must have a unique imagination. For example, he must imagine people are going to buy and read his joke book.

I am beginning to believe that the publishers had a conspiracy against me. Twenty of them refused this book. I asked one publisher if I should put more fire in my jokes. He said, "No, quite the reverse." I asked another publisher if he had read my last joke book. He replied, "I certainly hope so."

With such encouragement I turned to my best friend and asked him what he thought of my joke books. He told me he really appreciated them because the pages were just the size of his bird cage. I told him that was a fowl remark.

Because of the avid interest, many requests and tremendous encouragement from friends, I hereby present to the world . . . *More Good Clean Jokes.*

Bob Phillips

Table of Contents

BIBLE KNOWLEDGE

Teacher: Do you know who built the Ark?
Student: No.
Teacher: Correct.

*   *   *

Question: Why was Job always cold in bed?
Answer: Because he had such miserable comforters.

*   *   *

Sunday School teacher: What do you think the "land flowing with milk and honey: will be like?
Student: Sticky!

*   *   *

Question: What was the Tower of Babel?
Answer: Wasn't that where Solomon kept his wives?

*   *   *

"Did you know that Job spoke when he was a very small baby?"

"Where does it say that?"

"It says, 'Job cursed the day he was born.' "

*　　*　　*

Question: What is the strongest day in the week?

Answer: Sunday. The rest are weekdays.

*　　*　　*

Question: What does the story of Jonah and the great fish teach us?

Answer: You can't keep a good man down.

*　　*　　*

Question: Which came first, the chicken or the egg?

Answer: The chicken, of course. God couldn't lay an egg.

*　　*　　*

Noah was standing at the gangplank checking off the pairs of animals when he saw three camels trying to get on board.

"Wait a minute!" said Noah. "Two each is the limit. One of you will have to stay behind."

"It won't be me," said the first camel. "I'm the camel whose back is broken by the last straw."

"I'm the one people swallow while straining at a gnat," said the second.

"I," said the third, "am the one that shall pass through the eye of a needle sooner than a rich man shall enter heaven."

"Come on in," said Noah, "the world is going to need all of you."

*   *   *

Question: Do you know what the name of Isaiah's horse was?

Answer: Is Me. He said, "Woe, is me."

*   *   *

Baseball is talked about a great deal in the Bible:— In the big inning . . . —Eve stole first—Adam stole second—Gideon rattled the pitchers—Goliath was put out by David—Prodigal Son made a home run

*   *   *

The Bible must be the Word of God to withstand such poor preaching through the years.

*   *   *

Question: Where was deviled ham mentioned in the Bible?

Answer: When the evil spirits entered the swine.

*   *   *

THE CHOPPING BLOCK

He is a man with his feet firmly planted in mid-air.

*   *   *

"Do you know of any cures for insomnia?"
"Try talking to yourself."

*   *   *

That is a pretty suit. Too bad they didn't have it in your size.

*   *   *

"I'm chilled to the bone."
"Why don't you put on your hat?"

*   *   *

"I dread the thought of forty-five."
"Why? What happened to you then, dear?"

*   *   *

You can tell by his jokes he has a street-sweeper mind . . . always in the gutter.

*   *   *

"I have a bitter taste in my mouth."
"Been biting your tongue?"

*   *   *

"And what make you think he deserves the name Great Lover?"
"I watched him standing before a mirror."

*   *   *

Bill: I have had to make a living by my wits.
Gill: Well, half a living is better than none.

*   *   *

"And what brings you to town?"
"I just came to see the sights and I thought I'd call on you first."

*   *   *

"Something came into my mind just now and went away again."
"Maybe it was lonely."

*   *   *

"You should be ashamed of yourself, laughing at that fat man."
"I'm just having fun at his expanse."

*   *   *

Mary: My husband had my photograph over his heart during the war. In fact, it stopped a bullet one time and saved his life.
Jerri: I'm not surprised, dear. It would stop anything.

*   *   *

"I suppose you think I'm a perfect idiot."
"Oh, none of us is perfect."

*   *   *

She was a four-letter girl in college: D. U. M. B.

*   *   *

"Is it raining outside?"
"Did you ever see it raining inside?"

*   *   *

You've heard of Elvis the Pelvis? This is Kelly . . .

*   *   *

That's a very cute dress she almost has on.

*   *   *

The way she wears clothes, she can't even hide her embarrassment.

*   *   *

Every girl has the right to be ugly, but she abused the privilege.

*   *   *

She can easily protect herself from Peeping Toms. All she has to do is leave the shades up.

*   *   *

When he meets another egotist, it's an I for an I.

*   *   *

They call him Moses. It seems like every time he opens his mouth the bull rushes.

*   *   *

Why don't you sue your brains for nonsupport?

*   *   *

He has a small birthmark on his head . . . his brain.

*   *   *

"That singer has a terrible voice. Do you know who she is?"
"Yes, she is my wife."

"Well, I really didn't mean her voice, it is the music she has to sing. I wonder who wrote that awful music."

"I did."

*   *   *

He was so ugly when he was a baby they used to diaper his face.

*   *   *

Is that your face or did your neck throw up?

*   *   *

Him: When I stand on my head, the blood rushes to it. Why doesn't it rush to my feet when I stand up?

Her: That's because your feet aren't empty.

*   *   *

He is the kind of person that makes you wish birth control was retroactive.

*   *   *

Let's play horse. I'll be the front end . . . you just be yourself.

*   *   *

He's the kind of guy that can really creep into your heart and mind. In fact, you'll never meet a bigger creep!

*   *   *

That's all right mister. The original amateur hour is

tomorrow night. Tonight it's (name of program).

* * *

"She looks like she has been poured into her dress."
"Yeah, and forgot to say when."

* * *

She has delusions of glamour!

* * *

"I have never seen Joan look so pale."
"She was probably out in the rain without an umbrella."

* * *

Hokum: What do you mean by telling everyone I am deaf and dumb?
Yokum: That's not true. I never said you were deaf.

* * *

Jack: Aren't some of the clothes women wear absurd?
Frank: Yes. And yet, it looks so appropriate on some of them.

* * *

"Jim proposed to me last night."
"Doesn't he do it nicely?"

* * *

"You say there was something in her speech that sounded strange. What was that?"

"A pause."

* * *

Her idea of housework is to sweep the room with a glance.

* * *

You: "How much to you weigh?"
Heckler: "Oh, about 150 pounds."
You: "I'll bet 140 of that is *mouth*!"

* * *

She: You remind me of Don Juan.
He: (Flattered) Tell me just how.
She: Well, for one thing, he's been dead for years.

* * *

"I am a self-made man!"
"Why did you make yourself like THAT!"

* * *

"I am a self-made man!"
"Well, that relieves the Almighty of a great responsibility."

* * *

He is the kind of guy that would go to a home for the blind and pound the Braille flat.

* * *

"I simply can't bear idiots!"
"How odd . . . apparently your mother could."

*   *   *

"This oil makes my leg smart."
"Try rubbing it on your head."

*   *   *

"My opinion of you is a perfectly contemptible one."
"I never knew any opinion of yours, sir, which was not contemptible."

*   *   *

"I believe I could write like Shakespeare if I had a mind to try it."
"Yes, nothing is wanting but the mind!"

*   *   *

"Darling, how do you like my new outfit; It was made in London."
"Really? Did you swim back in it?"

*   *   *

"Our dog is just like one of the family."
"Really? Which one?"

*   *   *

"Everyone says I got my good looks from my father."
"Oh? Is he a plastic surgeon?"

*   *   *

"I don't think success has gone to her head."
"No, just to her mouth."

*   *   *

"I got a job working for a drug store. I'm supposed to increase business."
"What do you do? Stand out front and make people sick?"

*   *   *

"Has anyone ever told you how wonderful you are?
"Nope."
"Well, then, where did you get the idea?"

*   *   *

"Oh, I can't catch my breath."
"With your breath you should be thankful!"

*   *   *

"Not very funny, is he?"
"No, he couldn't even entertain a doubt."

*   *   *

"You know, you've changed since I saw you last."
"And how? For better or worse?"
"My dear, you could only change for the better."

*   *   *

"What would you say if I asked you to be my wife?"
"Nothing. I can't talk and laugh at the same time."

*   *   *

"I'm a lady killer."
"Yeah, they take one look at you and drop dead."

*   *   *

"I've been asked to get married lots of times."
"Who asked you?"
"Mother and father."

*   *   *

"Darling, I read your new book yesterday. I loved it. Who wrote it for you?"
"I'm glad you liked it. Who read it to you?"

*   *   *

"Oh, Sarah, I completely forgot about your little party last night."
"Weren't you there?"

*   *   *

"That's a beautiful rainbow tie you are wearing!"
"What do you mean by a 'rainbow tie?'"
"It has a big pot at the end!"

*   *   *

"Why darling, I was just wondering why you weren't invited to the party the Smith's had last week!"
"Isn't that a coincidence. I was just wondering why you were!"

*   *   *

"And do you know, I refused to marry Jim Mc

Manus a year ago, and he has been drinking ever since."

"Isn't that carrying a celebration a little too far?"

*   *   *

"And when I was sixteen, the President of the United States presented me a beauty award."

"Really? I didn't think Lincoln bothered with that sort of thing!"

*   *   *

"How do you like it? It's just a little something I threw on."

"Looks like you missed."

*   *   *

"What happened to that dopey blonde your husband used to run around with?"

"I dyed my hair!"

*   *   *

"Was that your wife I saw you with last night?"

"No, that was my son-in-law and I could cry every time I think about it."

*   *   *

"I don't look thirty-eight, do I?"

"Not anymore!"

*   *   *

Girl: You remind me of an ocean.

Boy: You mean wild . . . restless . . . and romantic?

Girl: No, you just make me sick.

* * *

"You know, girls, a lot of men are going to be miserable when I marry."

"Really? How many men are you going to marry?"

* * *

"I'm homesick! I'm homesick!"
"But you're at home!"
"I know . . . and I'm sick of it!"

* * *

At a supermarket a woman crowded ahead of another. "I hope you don't mind," said the woman carrying a can. "All I wanted was this cat food."

"Not at all," replied the other coolly. "You look hungry."

* * *

"I'd let those doctors experiment on me for the sake of science. I'm not afraid. I've gone through the war. Why I even once volunteered to let them put a new heart into my chest if one was available which suited my character."

"What was the matter? Couldn't they find a chicken big enough?"

* * *

"This lace is over sixty years old."
"Really? Over sixty years old? Did you make it yourself?"

* * *

"The President has personally asked me to help beautify the United States on a special project."

"Really? And which country have you decided to move to?"

* * *

"I'm getting divorced, girls!"

"Oh? Who's the lucky man?"

* * *

"Sam says I look like a million!"

"Yeah, all wrinkled and green."

* * *

"Harry, I have some good news for you and some bad news. First, I have decided to run off with Harvey White."

"Isn't that interesting. Now, tell me the bad news."

* * *

The two men entered the sumptuous house, and when they were alone one of them asked:

"Was that your wife who opened the door?"

"Of course it was," said the other. "You don't think I would hire a maid that ugly?"

* * *

She: Whenever some bore at a party asks me what I do for a living I say I'm a juggler with a circus.

He: And what do you do for a living?

She: I'm a juggler with a circus!

*   *   *

"I wish I was born in the Dark Ages."
"So do I. You look terrible in the light."

*   *   *

"I seem to be a rose between two thorns," remarked Miss Prettygirl as she seated herself between two men at a football game.

"I'd say it's more like a tongue sandwich," retorted one of the men.

*   *   *

What do you call frozen water?
Iced water.
What do you call frozen ink?
Iced ink.
You're telling me!

*   *   *

"Well, I must be going."

"Don't let me keep you if you really must be going," said his bored host.

"Yes, I really must go. But, really, I did enjoy our little visit. Do you know, when I came in here I had a headache but now I have lost it entirely."

"Oh, it isn't lost," was the patient reply. "I've got it now."

*   *   *

A tired guest at a formal function spoke to the man next to him:

"Gee, this thing is a bore; I'm going to beat it!"

"I would, too," said the man, "but I've got to stay. I'm the host!"

*　　*　　*

"Don't bother showing me to the door."
"It's no bother . . . it's a pleasure!"

*　　*　　*

"Your not smart enough to talk to an idiot!"
"Okay! I'll send you a letter!"

*　　*　　*

"Thank goodness that misery is over!"
"What misery?"
"Talking with the hostess. Have you been through it yet?"
"I don't have to. I'm the host."

*　　*　　*

"When I got on the bus three men got up to give me their seats."
"Did you take them?"

*　　*　　*

"Is this one of your silly abstract paintings?"
"No, that's a mirror!"

*　　*　　*

"Did you see that young lady smile at me?"
"That's nothing. The first time I saw you, I laughed right our loud."

*　　*　　*

"I kissed her under the mistletoe."
"I wouldn't kiss her under anesthetic!"

"Sir, how dare you belch before my wife!"
"Sorry, ol' pal. I didn't know it was her turn!"

*   *   *

Clara: My husband says I look younger in this hat.
Sara: Oh, really? What is your age?
Clara. Thirty.
Sara: No, I mean without the hat!

*   *   *

Postlude
To guests he is the gracious host,
To children three he is "the most,"
To loving wife the perfect mate,
To fellow workers he's "just great!"

How SAD then that a humble friend
Upon his promise can't depend,
From east to west, from north to south,
His name? You guessed it! *BLABBERMOUTH!!*

DATING GAME

Here is your engagement ring.
She: But this diamond has a flaw in it.
He: You shouldn't notice that . . . we are in love
and love is blind.
She: Not stone blind.

*   *   *

Father: How dare you! What do you mean by hugging my daughter?

Boy: I—I—I— was just carrying out the scriptural injunction, "hold fast that which is good."

* * *

Her: Will you love me when I am old?

He: I will love you. I will cherish the ground you walk upon. I will . . . You won't look like your mother, will you?

* * *

A bride is a woman with a fine prospect of happiness behind her.

* * *

"Bill told me I was the only girl he ever loved."

"Doesn't he say it beautifully?"

* * *

He: If you would give me your phone number I would give you a call.

She: It's in the book.

He: Good. What is your name?

She: It's in the book, too.

* * *

"I hear the groom ran away from the altar."

"Lost his nerve, I suppose?"

"No, found it again."

* * *

After a Dutch-treat-on-everything date, the girl

responded to her escort who brought her home:
"Since we've gone Dutch on everything else, you can
just kiss yourself goodnight!"

*   *   *

Bachelors know more about women than married
men; if they didn't, they'd be married, too.

*   *   *

He: Will you marry me?
She: No.
And they lived happily ever after!

*   *   *

Him: If I tried to kiss you, would you call for
help?
Her: Do you need help?

*   *   *

Jean: When are you thinking about getting married?
Joan: Constantly.

*   *   *

She: You finally asked Daddy for my hand in
marriage. What did he say?
He: Not a word. He just fell on my neck and
sobbed.

*   *   *

"If you refuse to marry me I will die," said the
young romantic. And, sure enough, fifty years later
he died.

*   *   *

Girl: Would you like to take a walk?
Boy: I'd love to.
Girl: Well, don't let me detain you.

*   *   *

"She thinks no man is good enough for her."
"She may be right."
"She may be left."

*   *   *

Conceited: "I can tell just by looking into a girl's eyes exactly how she feels about me."
Girl: "Gee, that must be embarrassing for you."

*   *   *

Him: There is one word that will make me the happiest man in the world. Will you marry me?
Her: No!
Him: That's the word!

*   *   *

Bill: "I think I'm in love."
Pete: "Really?"
Bill: "Yes. All I need to do is find a girl."

*   *   *

Boy: I guess you've been out with worse looking fellows than I am, haven't you?
Boy: I guess you've been out with worse looking fellows than I am, haven't you?
Girl: I heard you the first time. I was just trying to think.

*　　*　　*

Boy: I would like to marry you.

Girl: Well, leave your name and address and if nothing better turns up, I will notify you.

*　　*　　*

Boy: You look prettier every minute. Do you know what that is a sign of?

Girl: Yes, you are about to run out of gas.

*　　*　　*

Boy: I want to be honest. You're not the first girl I've kissed.

Girl: I want to be honest. You've got a lot to learn.

*　　*　　*

Boy: You could learn to love me, couldn't you?

Girl: Well, I learned to eat spinach.

FOOD FOR THOUGHT

Customer: I am sorry, waiter, but I only have enough money for the bill. I have nothing left for a tip.

Waiter: Let me add up that bill again, sir.

*　　*　　*

Eat, drink and be merry for tomorrow we diet.

*　　*　　*

Someday I would like to see a waiter with enough courage to lay the check face up on the table.

*   *   *

Some people are no good at counting calories and they have the figures to prove it.

*   *   *

Customer: One of the claws on this lobster is missing.
Waiter: They fight in the kitchen and sometimes bite each other's claws off.
Customer: Then take this one back and bring me a winner.

*   *   *

Waiter: We have a very up to date place here. Everything is cooked by electricity.
Customer: I wonder if you would mind giving this steak another shock?

*   *   *

Customer: I'll have some raw oysters, not too large nor too small, not too salty nor too fat. They must be cold and I want them quickly!
Waiter: Yes, sir! With or without pearls?

*   *   *

Customer: Would you mind taking the fly out of my soup?
Waiter: Do it yourself. I'm no lifeguard.

*   *   *

Customer: This coffee tastes like mud.

Waiter: Well, it was ground this morning.

*   *   *

Customer in a hurry: Will the hotcakes be long?
Cook: No, round, as usual.

*   *   *

Man: There's a splinter in my cottage cheese!
Waiter: What do you expect for fifty-five cents
. . . the whole cottage?

*   *   *

A man took his 10-year-old son to an elegant restaurant and was surprised to hear him order the usual hamburger. "Try something different and unusual," he urged him.

"I am," he hispered. "I never had a three-dollar hamburger before!"

*   *   *

Calories don't count . . . they multiply and divide all over the body.

*   *   *

"I never eat any food with additives. I don't eat anything with preservatives or anything that's been sprayed or anything that's been fed chemical grain."

"And how do you feel?"

"Hungry."

*   *   *

SPECIAL REDUCING DIET

MONDAY
   Breakfast—Weak tea
   Lunch—1 bouillon cube in ½ cup diluted water
   Dinner—1 pigeon thigh & 2 oz. prune juice (gargle
      only)

TUESDAY
   Breakfast—Scraped crumbs from burned toast
   Lunch—1 doughnut hole (without sugar)
   Dinner—2 jellyfish skins & 1 glass dehydrated
      water

WEDNESDAY
   Breakfast—boiled out stains from table cover
   Lunch—½ doz. poppy seeds
   Dinner—Bees knees & mosquito knuckles sauteed
      with vinegar

THURSDAY
   Breakfast—Shredded eggshell skins
   Lunch—Bellybutton from a naval orange
   Dinner—3 eyes from Irish potatoes (diced)

FRIDAY
   Breakfast—2 lobster antennae1 guppy fin
   Lun ch—1 guppy fin
   Dinner—jellyfish vertabrae a la book binders

SATURDAY
   Breakfast—4 chopped banana seeds
   Lunch—Broiled butterfly liver
   Dinner—Fillet of soft shell crab slaw

SUNDAY
   Breakfast—Pickled humming bird tongue
   Lunch—Prime ribs of tadpole & aroma of empty
      custard pie plate
   Dinner—Tossed paprika & clover leaf (1) salad

NOTE: All meals to be eaten under microscope to avoid extra portion.

HELP! POLICE!

Robber: I'm going to shoot you.
Man: Why?
Robber: I shoot anyone who looks like me.
Man: Do I look like you?
Robber: Yes.
Man: Then shoot.

*　　　*　　　*

Judge: Haven't I seen you before?
Man: Yes, Your Honor. I taught your daughter how to play the piano.
Judge: Thirty years.

.　*　　　*　　　*

Judge: What good have you ever done for society?
Robber: Well, I've kept four or five detectives working regularly.

*　　　*　　　*

Policeman: In the gun battle a bullet struck my head and went into space.
Wife: Well, at least you're honest.

*　　　*　　　*

Policeman: How did this accident happen?
Motorist: My wife fell asleep in the back seat.

* * *

Crime is so bad in my neighborhood we have the only police station in town that's insured against burglary.

* * *

Speeder: But, Judge, I do everything fast.
Judge: Let's see how fast you can do thirty days.

* * *

Things are getting so bad in my neighborhood that one gangster does all his holdups in daylight. He's afraid to be out on the street at night with all that money.

* * *

"Couldn't you get that crook to confess to the crime?" asked the police chief.
"We tried everything, sir. We browbeat and badgered him with every question we could think of."
"How did he respond?"
"He just dozed off and said now and then: 'Yes, dear. You are perfectly right.' "

* * *

Sign at a traffic court:
DON'T COMPLAIN, THINK OF THE SUMMONSES YOU HAVE DESERVED BUT DIDN'T GET!

* * *

Policeman: Name, please.
Motorist: Wilhem Von Corquerinski Popolavawitz.

27

Policeman: Well, don't let me catch you speeding again.

*   *   *

John Smith happened to witness a minor holdup. In due time, the police arrived and one officer asked the witness his name.

"John Smith," said Smith.

"Cut the comedy," snapped the cop. "What's your real name?"

"All right," said Smith, "put me down as Winston Churchill."

"That's more like it," said the officer. "You can't fool me with that Smith stuff."

*   *   *

Robber: Give me all your money.

Citizen: All I have is a watch and it only has sentimental value.

Robber: Fork it over. I feel like a good cry.

*   *   *

"What happened to your nose?"

"I got into an argument with a man about driving in traffic."

"Why didn't you call a policeman?"

"He was a policeman."

*   *   *

Policeman: What are you doing?

Man: Committing suicide.

Policeman: Why do you have the rope around your middle instead of your neck?

Man: I tried it around my neck and I couldn't breathe.

*　　　*　　　*

Judge: Thirty years in prison!
Prisoner: But, Judge, I won't live that long!
Judge: Don't worry, do what you can.

*　　　*　　　*

Policeman: Did you get the license number of the car that knocked you down, madam?
Woman: No, but the driver was wearing a three-piece tweed suit lined with pink crepe, and she had on a perwinkle hat trimmed with red roses.

*　　　*　　　*

"How did you come to join the Police Department?"
"I've always wanted to be in a business where it's the customer whose always wrong."

*　　　*　　　*

"My uncle is in Leavenworth because he made big money."
"How much?"
"About a third of an inch too big."

*　　　*　　　*

IN THE BEGINNING

Question: At what season did Eve eat the fruit?
Answer: Early in the fall.

*　　　*　　　*

Question: What is that which Adam never saw or possessed, yet left two for each of his children.
Answer: Parents.

* * *

Question: How were Adam and Eve prevented from gambling?
Answer: Their paradise (pair-o-dice) was taken away from them.

* * *

Even Adam and Eve had their problems. One day Adam got angry. "You've done it again, Eve," said Adam. "You put my shirt in the salad again."

* * *

Bill: What was Eve's telephone number in the Garden of Eden?
Jill: I think it was Adam-812.

* * *

Question: What nationality were Adam and Eve?
Answer: Soviet citizens, of course . . . nothing to wear, only an apple to eat but living in Paradise.

* * *

IN THE SERVICE

During the Israeli Six-Day War, five Arabs pounced on an Israeli soldier who proceeded to beat the devil out of them. As the Arabs ran away, the Israeli soldier shouted after them, "You're lucky my husband isn't here to catch you."

*   *   *

"What did you do in the Army?"
"I was an eye doctor. My job was to cut the eyes out of potatoes."

*   *   *

Officer: Are you happy now that you're in the Army?
Soldier: Yes, sir.
Officer: What were you before you got into the Army?
Soldier: Much happier.

*   *   *

A soldier who lost his rifle was reprimanded by his captain and told he would have to pay for it.
"Sir," gulped the soldier, "suppose I lost a tank. Surely I would not have to pay for that!"
"Yes, you would, too," bellowed the captain, "even if it took the rest of your life."
"Well," said the soldier, "now I know why the captain goes down with his ship."

*   *   *

The recruiting officer was at work on the young man. "Don't you want to join the cavalry?" he said. "That's a fine branch of the service."
"No, sir," said the man. "If I had to retreat, I don't want to be bothered by dragging a horse behind me."

*   *   *

Two sailors were adrift on a raft in the ocean. They had just about given up hope of rescue. One began to pray, "O Lord, I've led a worthless life. I've been unkind to my wife and I've neglected my children, but if you'll save me, I promise . . . "

The other shouted, "Hold it. I think I see land."

*　　*　　*

The new Army recruit was given guard duty at 2 a.m. He did his best for awhile but about 4 a.m. he went to sleep. He awakened to find the officer of the day standing before him.

Remembering the heavy penalty for being asleep on guard duty, this smart young man kept his head bowed for another moment, then looked upward and reverently said, "A-a-a-a-men!"

*　　*　　*

A young naval student was being put through the paces by an old sea captain. "What would you do if a sudden storm sprang up on the starboard?"

"Throw out an anchor, sir."

"What would you do if another storm sprang up aft?"

"Throw out another anchor, sir."

"And if another terrific storm sprang up forward, what would you do?"

"Throw out another anchor."

"Hold on," said the Captain, "where are you getting all those anchors from?"

"From the same place you're getting your storms, sir."

*　　*　　*

A small boy was leading a donkey by an Army camp. A couple of soldiers wanted to have some fun with the boy.

"Why are you holding on to your brother so tight for?" one of them said.

"So he won't join the Army," was the reply.

*   *   *

FAMILY FRENZY

Mother: Judy, I have told you before not to speak when older people are talking. Wait until they stop.

Judy: I tried, but they never stop.

*   *   *

Father: Sue, what are you doing out there?

Sue: I'm looking at the moon.

Father: Well, tell the moon to go home. It's half-past eleven.

*   *   *

Billy: Mrs. Wilson, may I look at your rug?

Mrs. Wilson: Why, of course, Billy. Come in.

Billy: I don't understand . . . it doesn't make me sick.

*   *   *

A wife got lost on one of her driving lessons. "What should I do?" she said to her husband.

"Just imagine that I was driving and do what you'd say I should do."

*   *   *

"How long did it take your wife to learn to drive a car?"

"It will be thirteen years this May."

*   *   *

Son: Dad's birthday is tomorrow. What should we get for him?

Daughter: Maybe we should let him have his car for a change.

*   *   *

One of the great mysteries of life is how that idiot who married your daughter can be the father of the smartest grandchildren in the world.

*   *   *

"Daddy, before you married Mommy, who told you how to drive?"

*   *   *

Mother: If a young man asks you for a kiss, refuse it.

Daughter: And if he doesn't ask for it?

*   *   *

Mother: Your hairdo looks like a mop.

Daughter: What's a mop?

*   *   *

An old Chinaman was eating too much rice especially since he was too frail to work. Because the grandfather had become a burden, the father of the home, his son, determined to get rid of him. He put him in a wheelbarrow, then started up the mountain. The little eight-year-old grandson went along. He was full of questions. His father explained that the grandfather was old and useless and the only thing they could do was to take him up the mountain and leave him to die. Then the grandson had a bright idea. "I'm glad you brought me along, Father, because when you're old, I'll know where to take you."

*   *   *

Neighbor: How is your son doing in college?
Father: Well, I felt like Aaron did in the wilderness. "Behold, I poured in the gold and there came out this calf."

*   *   *

Father: Now, remember, I'm spanking you because I love you.
Son: I sure wish I was big enough to return your love.

*   *   *

"It is no fair, Mom. Johnny has the largest piece of cake. It is unfair. He was eating cake two years before I was born."

*   *   *

Husband: I know you are having a lot of trouble with the baby, dear, but keep in mind, "the hand that rocks the cradle is the hand that rules the world."
Wife: How about taking over the world for a few hours while I go shopping?

*   *   *

My husband is on a seafood diet. Every time he sees food, he eats.

* * *

Mother: I don't think the man upstairs likes Mike to play on his drums.

Father: Why do you say that?

Mother: Because this afternoon he gave Mike a knife and asked him if he knew what was inside the drum.

* * *

Babysitter: Johnny swallowed a cricket.

Mother: Oh, my! Did you call the doctor?

Babysitter: I didn't need to. I gave him some insect powder.

* * *

A boy watching his dad bury a cat that had been hit by a car said, "It won't do any good. It won't grow."

* * *

Son: Why do the ladies always bring their knitting when they come to visit?

Father: So they will have something to think about while they talk.

* * *

Little Susan was mother's helper. She helped set the table when company was due for dinner. Presently everything was on, the guest came in and everyone sat down. Then mother notices something was missing. "Susan," she said, "You didn't put a knife and fork at Mr. Larson's place."

"I thought he wouldn't need them " explained Susan. "Daddy said he always eats like a horse."

*　　*　　*

Dad came home from work just before supper and his five-year-old daughter met him on the sidewalk. She was not smiling so he asked why. "Is something wrong, honey?" he asked.

"Yes, all day long I've been having trouble with your wife."

*　　*　　*

"Do you know that Joe beats his wife up every morning?"

"Really?"

"Yes, he gets up at 6:00 a.m. and she gets up at 7:30 a.m."

*　　*　　*

"Does your mother spank you?"

"Yes."

"Does your daddy spank you?

"Yes."

"Who hurts the most?"

"I do."

*　　*　　*

Pete: Mother, you gave brother a bigger piece of cake than you gave me.

Mother: But, sweetheart, your brother is a much bigger boy than you are.

Pete: Well, he always will be if this keeps up.

*　　*　　*

"I hear your husband is a linguist."

"Yes. He speaks three languages . . . golf, football, and baseball."

37

*   *   *

"I'm supposed to tell you that there will be a small Parent-Teachers meeting tomorrow night," said the boy to his dad.

"Well, if it's going to be small, do I have to go?" asked the father.

"Oh, yes," replied the son. "It's just you, me, the teacher and the principal."

*   *   *

Dad: How dare you kick your little brother in the stomach.

Son: It's his own fault, Daddy. He turned around.

*   *   *

Son: How do they catch lunatics, Dad?

Dad: With lipstick, beautiful dresses and pretty smiles.

*   *   *

Daughter: Mom, may I have some money for a new dress?

Mother: Ask your father, dear. You are getting married in a month and the practice would do you good.

*   *   *

Wife: Would you help me with the dishes?

Husband: That isn't a man's job.

Wife: The Bible suggests that it is.

Husband: Where does it say that?

Wife: In II Kings 21:13 it says, " . . . And I will wipe Jerusalem as a man wipeth a dish, wiping it and turning it upside down."

*　　*　　*

Mother: Eat your spinach. Think of the thousands of starving children who would love some spinach like this.

Billy: Name two.

*　　*　　*

Young man: Do you mind being old?

Old man: Oh, it's not so bad when you consider the alternative.

*　　*　　*

You can tell how old you are by remembering when a family went for a Sunday drive and everyone got in the same car.

*　　*　　*

"What do you think of your new little brother, dear?"

"I wish we'd thrown him away and kept the stork instead."

*　　*　　*

Mother: Eat your spinach, dear. It makes strong teeth.

Son: Why don't you feed it to Grandpa?

*　　*　　*

Father: When I was your age, I never kissed a girl. Will you be able to tell your children that?

Son: Not with a straight face.

*　　*　　*

Boy: I'd like to marry your daughter.

Father: Have you seen my wife yet?

Boy: I have . . . but I prefer your daughter.

* * *

Mother: Why did you spank Billy? What did he do?

Father: Nothing, but tomorrow he gets his report and I'll be out of town.

* * *

Jack: My wife used to play the piano a lot, but since the children came she doesn't have time.

Mack: Children are a comfort, aren't they?

* * *

When Joe was a little boy, he took fiddle lessons. One day while he was practicing, scraping dismally back and forth with his bow, his dog set up a plaintive wailing and howling. Finally Joan, who was trying to do her homework, stuck her head into the room where her brother was practicing.

"For goodness sake!" she complained. "Can't you play something the dog doesn't know?"

* * *

Betty: Did your mother promise you anything if you do the dishes?

Sue: No, but she promised me something if I didn't.

* * *

Husband: Dear me, where are my golf socks?

Wife: What golf socks?

Husband: The ones that have eighteen holes in them.

*   *   *

Daughter: Oh, Mother, please tell me if I should accept Joe's proposal.
Mother: Why don't you ask your father? He made a much smarter decision in marriage than I did.

*   *   *

Son: Why do they refer to nature as a woman, dad?
Father: Because they can't find out how old it is, son.

*   *   *

Barber: You're next.
Long-haired teenager: I'm not waiting for a haircut. My father is looking for me and this is the last place he'd expect to find me.

*   *   *

"I'm really worried."
"Why?"
"Well, my wife read *The Tale of Two Cities* and we had twins. Later she read *The Three Musketeers* and we had triplets. Now she is reading *Birth Of A Nation*!"

*   *   *

Husband: And here is an eggplant.
Wife: When will the eggs be ripe?

*   *   *

A garage sale is a technique for distributing all the junk in your garage among all the other garages in the neighborhood.

*   *   *

We've just moved into our dream house. It costs twice as much as we ever dreamed it would.

*   *   *

Father: What good is the steam that comes out of the spout on the kettle when it boils?

Son: So that mother can open your letter before you get home.

*   *   *

A mother, visiting a department store took her son to the toy department. Spying a gigantic rocking horse he climbed up on it and rocked back and forth for almost an hour.

"Come on, son," the mother pleaded. "I have to get home to get father's dinner."

The little lad refused to budge and all her efforts were unavailing. The department manager also tried to coax the little fellow without meeting with any success. Eventually, in desperation they called the store's psychiatrist. Gently he walked over and whispered a few words in the boys ear and immediately the lad jumped off and ran to his mother's side.

"How did you do it?" the mother asked incredibly. "What did you say to him?"

The psychiatrist hesitated for a moment, then said, "All I said was, 'If you don't jump off that rocking horse at once, son, I'll knock the stuffing out of you!"

*   *   *

Son: What is a monologue, Dad?

Dad: That's a conversation between a man and a wife.

Son: But our teacher said that was a dialogue.

Dad: Your teacher isn't married, son.

*　　*　　*

Son: Dad, you wouldn't spank me for something I didn't do, would you?

Father: Why, of course not.

Son: Good! I didn't do my homework.

*　　*　　*

THE DEFENDERS

Witness: Well I think . . .

Lawyer: Don't think! In this court room you are to tell what you know, not what you think!

Witness: Well, I'm not a lawyer. I can't talk without thinking!

*　　*　　*

"And what do you do, sir?"

"I'm a criminal lawyer."

"Aren't they all!"

*　　*　　*

Mrs. Franklin had been called for jury duty. She declined to serve because, she said, she did not believe in capital punishment. The judge tried to persuade her to stay. "Madam," he said, "this is not a murder case. It is merely a case in which a wife is suing her husband because she gave him $4,000 to buy her a new fur coat and he lost it all at the race track instead."

"I'll serve," agreed Mrs. Franklin. "I could be wrong about capital punishment."

*　　*　　*

Counsel: Do you wish to challenge any of the jury?

Prisoner: Well, I think I could lick that little fellow on this end.

*　　*　　*

GOOD MEDICINE

Chinese eye doctor: It looks like you have a cataract.

Patient: No, it is a Rincoln Continental.

*　　*　　*

Young doctor: What is the secret of your success?

Old doctor: Always write your prescriptions illegibly and your bills very plainly.

*　　*　　*

Doctors tell us there are over 7 million people who are overweight. These, of course, are only round figures.

*　　*　　*

Patient: Do you think raw oysters are healthy?

Doctor: I've never heard one complain.

*   *   *

He's so nervous, he keeps coffee awake.

*   *   *

"Did you say the man was shot in the woods, doctor?"
"No, I said he was shot in the lumbar region."

*   *   *

Doctor: Did you tell Mr. Smith that he is the father of triplets?
Nurse: No, he is still shaving.

*   *   *

"Who is that strange looking man who keeps staring at me?"
"Oh, that is Mr. Marconi, the famous expert on insanity."

*   *   *

Wife: My husband thinks he's a refrigerator.
Psychiatrist: I wouldn't worry as long as he is not violent.
Wife: Oh, the delusion doesn't bother me. But when he sleeps with his mouth open, the little light keeps me awake.

*   *   *

Wife: My husband frightens me the way he blows smoke rings through his nose.
Psychiatrist: That isn't unusual.
Wife: But my husband doesn't smoke.

45

*　　*　　*

Patient: I've got butterflies in my stomach.
Doctor: Did you try an aspirin?
Patient: Yes and they are playing ping pong with it.

*　　*　　*

Neurotics build air castles. Psychotics live in them. Psychiatrists collect the rent.

*　　*　　*

As a patient came slowly out of the anesthetic he said, "Why are the blinds drawn, doctor?"
"There's a fire across the street and we didn't want you to think the operation was a failure."

*　　*　　*

Doctor: I have some good news and some bad news.
Patient: What is the bad news?
Doctor: We had to cut off both of your legs.
Patient: What is the good news?
Doctor: There is a woman upstairs that would like to buy your shoes.

*　　*　　*

She: What kind of doctor are you?
He: A naval surgeon.
She: My, how you doctors specialize.

*　　*　　*

"The other doctor and I disagree on your case. But I am sure that the autopsy will prove that I'm right."

*   *   *

Anyone who goes to a psychiatrist ought to have his head examined!

*   *   *

I'm glad I attended your lecture on insomnia, doctor.
"Did you find it interesting?"
"No, but it cured my insomnia."

*   *   *

"I just found out your uncle's an undertaker. I thought you told me he was a doctor."
"Nope, I just said he followed the medical profession."

*   *   *

The sad, quiet, big-eyed little lady sat in the psychiatrist's office. The good doctor questioned her gently as to why her family wanted her locked up.
"Now, tell me," he said, "just what your trouble is."
"It's just that . . . .just that I'm so fond of pancakes, doctor."
"Is that all? Why, I'm very fond of pancakes myself."
"Oh, doctor, really? You must come over to our house. I've got trunks and trunks full of them!"

*   *   *

Patient: Doctor, what I need is something to stir me up. Something to put in fighting trim. Did you put anything like that in this prescription?
Doctor: No. You will find that in the bill.

47

*   *   *

Joe: I'm afraid I can't afford that operation now.
Moe: It looks like you'll have to talk about your old one for another year.

*   *   *

"I have a cold or something in my head."
"I bet it's a cold."

*   *   *

The best way to cure your wife of nerves is to tell her it's caused by advancing age.

*   *   *

Doc: Could you pay for an operation if I thought one was necessary?
Patient: Would you think one was necessary if I couldn't pay for it?

*   *   *

When the farmer was admitted into the doctor's office, he mumbled, "Shore hope I'm sick."
The doctor said, "That certainly is a poor attitude!"
"Y'see, doc," replied the farmer, "I'd hate to feel like this if I'm well."

*   *   *

A toast for the Hay Fever Club . . . Here's looking at-chooooooooo!

*   *   *

Doctor: I can do nothing for your sickness. It is hereditary.

Patient: Then send the bill to my father.

* * *

My doctor doesn't believe in acupuncture. He'd rather stick you with his bill.

* * *

I'M FINE

I'm fine, I'm fine.
There's nothing whatever the matter with me,
I'm just as healthy as I can be.
I have arthritis in both of my knees
And when I talk, I talk with a wheeze.
My pulse is weak and my blood is thin
But I'm awfully well for the shape I'm in.
My teeth eventually will have to come out
And I can't hear a word unless you shout.
I'm overweight and I can't get thin
But I'm awfully well for the shape I'm in.
Arch supports I have for my feet
Or I wouldn't be able to walk down the street.
Sleep is denied me every night
And every morning I'm really a sight.
My memory is bad and my head's a-spin
And I practically live on aspirin.
But I'm awfully well for the shape I'm in.
The moral is, as this tale unfolds,
That for you and me who are growing old,
It's better to say, "I'm fine," with a grin
Than to let people know the shape we're in!

* * *

.... SO YOU THINK YOU HAVE TROUBLES!
When I got to the building, I found that the

hurrican had knocked some bricks off the top. So I rigged up a beam with a pulley at the top of the building and hoisted up a couple of barrels full of bricks. When I had fixed the building, there were a lot of bricks left over. Then I went to the bottom of the building, and cast off the line. Unfortunately, the barrel of bricks was heavier than I was, and before I knew what was happening, the barrel started down, jerking me off the ground.

I decided to hang on and halfway up I met the barrel coming down and received a hard blow on the shoulder. I then continued to the top, banging my head against the beam and getting my fingers jammed in the pulley. When the barrel hit the ground it burst its bottom, allowing all the bricks to spill out.

I was now heavier than the barrel and so started down again at high speed. Halfway down I met the barrel coming up and received more injuries to my shins.

When I hit the ground, I landed on the bricks, getting several painful cuts. At this point I must have lost my presence of mind because I let go the line. The barrel came down, giving me another heavy blow on the head and putting me in the hospital.

I respectfully request sick leave.

* * *

MY WIFE

Joe: My wife has been using a flesh reducing roller for nearly two months.

Moe: Can you see any results?

Joe: Yes, the roller is much thinner.

* * *

"I wouldn't say my wife is a poor housekeeper, but she doesn't turn on the stove. She just lights the grease."

*　　*　　*

Customer: I've come back to buy that television I was looking at yesterday.
Salesman: That's good. May I ask what the one dominating thing was that made you want this set?
Customer: My wife.

*　　*　　*

I don't know what to get my wife anymore. First she wanted a mink; I got her a mink. Then she wanted a silver fox; I got her a silver fox. It was ridiculous .. the house was full of animals.

*　　*　　*

My wife just had plastic surgery . . . I took away all her credit cards.

*　　*　　*

To give you an idea how difficult my wife can be, she bought me two ties for my birthday. To please her, I wore one. She yelled, "What's the matter? Don't you like the other one?"

*　　*　　*

The way my wife looks in the morning! She ran after the garbage man and said, "Am I too late for the garbage?"
He said, "No, jump in."

*　　*　　*

My wife talks so much I get hoarse just listening to her.

* * *

My wife is the sweetest, most tolerant, most beautiful woman in the world. This is a paid political announcement.

* * *

I walked into a store and said, "This is my wife's birthday. I'd like to buy her a beautiful fountain pen."

The clerk winked at me and said, "A little surprise, eh?"

I said, "Yes, she's expecting a Cadillac."

* * *

"My wife always has the last word."
"You're lucky. Mine never gets to it."

* * *

One day my wife drove up the side of a building and there was another woman driver coming down.

* * *

"Every once in awhile my wife puts on one of those mud packs."
"Does it improve her looks?"
"Only for a few days . . . then the mud falls off!"

* * *

"Why are you adding up those figures?"
"My wife said she is going to lose four pounds a

month. I figure that in 18 months I'll be rid of her!"

* * *

My wife thinks she's Teddy Roosevelt. She runs from store to store, yelling, "CHARGE!"

* * *

"My wife has been cooking a chicken for two days."
"For two days?"
"Yeah! The cookbook said to cook it one-half-hour to the pound ... and my wife weighs 110 pounds!"

* * *

Bob: My wife treats me like an idol.
Ray: Why do you say that?
Bob: She feeds me burnt offerings at meals.

* * *

"My wife says if I don't chuck golf, she'll leave me!"
"That's too bad."
"Yes, I'll miss her."

* * *

When we first married my wife was not a very good cook. She would make new desserts and have me try them before dinner.

One day I came home and she told me that she had just made a pumpkin pie. She told me to try some. I said, "How about after dinner?" She said, "No, I want you to try it now."

I don't want to say it was bad, but I had to drink four glassfuls!

*   *   *

I miss my wife's cooking . . . as often as I can.

*   *   *

My wife's meals are something to behold . . . not to eat, just behold.

*   *   *

My wife had a terrible accident in the kitchen the other night . . . and I ate it!

*   *   *

Joe: My wife is very touchy. The least little thing will set her off.
Moe: You're lucky. Mine is a self-starter.

*   *   *

My wife spends a fortune on cold creams and oils, puts them all over her body. I went to grab her, she slid out of bed.

*   *   *

My wife and I just celebrated our Tin Anniversary . . . 12 years eating out of cans.

*   *   *

My wife will never find where I hid my extra money. I hit it in my socks that need mending!

*   *   *

"Why are you so sad, Bill?"

"My wife said she wouldn't talk to me for thirty days."

"Why should that make you sad?"

"Today is her last day!"

*　　　*　　　*

"My wife is always asking for money," complained a man to his friend. "Last week she wanted $200. The day before yesterday she asked me for $125. This morning she wanted $150."

"That's crazy," said the friend. "What does she do with it all?"

"I don't know," said the man, "I never give her any."

*　　　*　　　*

My wife puts cold cream on at night, an inch thick. Then she puts those curlers in her hair, puts a fishing net over the whole thing and says, "Kiss me." I said, "Take me to your leader."

*　　　*　　　*

I came home last night and there was the car in the dining room.

I said to my wife, "How did you get the car in the dining room?"

She said, "It was easy. I made a left turn when I came out of the kitchen."

*　　　*　　　*

My wife likes those little foreign cars. I bought her two . . . one for each foot.

*　　　*　　　*

My wife changes her hair so many times she has sort of a convertible top.

*   *   *

"I try to do everything to make my wife happy. She complained about the housework so I bought her an electric iron, an electric dishwasher, and an electric dryer. Then she complained there were so many gadgets around the house she had no room to sit down. What could I do?"

"Buy her an electric chair!"

*   *   *

ODDS AND ENDS

"Could you tell me how you became such a rich man?"

"Turn out the lights and I will tell you the story."

"You need not tell the story. I think I already know."

*   *   *

"Doctor," she said loudly, bouncing into the room, "I want you to say frankly what's wrong with me."

He surveyed her from head to foot. "Madam," he said at length, "I've just three things to tell you.

"First, your weight needs to be reduced by nearly sixty pounds.

"Second, your beauty would be improved if you used one tenth as much rouge and lipstick.

"And, third, I'm an artist . . . the doctor lives on the next floor."

*   *   *

In a small town everyone made fun of a local misfit. They would hold out a dime and a nickel to him and ask him which he wanted. He would always choose a nickel. One day someone asked him why he always chose the nickel. The misfit replied, "If I ever took a dime, they'd quit giving me nickels."

*   *   *

Two men drove their cars toward each other on a narrow street. Neither could pass. One leaned out and shouted, "I never back up for a stupid idiot!"

"I always do!" shouted the other man, shifting into reverse.

*   *   *

"Is Mrs. Wilson an active member of your sewing circle?"

"Goodness, no!" She never says a word. Just sits there and sews."

*   *   *

A Scotsman and an Englishman were leaning against the counter in a store when a bandit walked in and brandished his gun.

The Scot, a quick thinker, hauled out his money and handed it to his English friend.

He said, "Here's the ten dollars you lent me."

*   *   *

Man: How far is it to the next filling station?
Farmer: Nigh onto two miles as the crow flies.
Man: Well, how far is it if the crow has to talk and roll a flat tire?

*   *   *

Middle age is when all one's energy goes to waist.

*   *   *

Attendant: Do you wish to consult with Wing Tong Fong, the great Chinese mystic?
Lady: Yes, tell him his mother is here from the Bronx.

*   *   *

Pat: I never have any trouble with back seat drivers. I never hear a word from behind.
Mike: What do you drive?
Pat: A hearse.

*   *   *

Red: I'd give a thousand dollars to anyone who would do my worrying for me.
Ted: You're on. Where's the thousand?
Red: That's your first worry.

*   *   *

"Will you lend me $20.00 and only give me ten of them? That way you will owe me ten, and I'll owe you ten, and we'll be straight."

*   *   *

With the Women's Lib movement coming in so strong, one cereal company had to change their advertisement to, "SNAP, CRACKLE and MOM."

*   *   *

The seven ages of a woman are baby, child, girl, young woman, young woman, young woman and poised social leader.

*   *   *

Our forefathers did without sugar until the 13th century, without coal fires until the 14th, without buttered bread until the 16th, tea or soap until the 17th, without gas, matches or electricity until the 19th, without cars, canned or frozen foods until the 20th. Now, what was it you were complaining about?

*   *   *

Two goats in the desert found a tin can full of film. One of them nuzzled it until the lid came off. The film leader loosened around the spool, and the goat ate a few frames.

The second goat ate some, too. Soon they pulled all the film off the reel and consumed the whole of it.

When nothing was left but the can and the spool, the first goat said, "Wasn't that great?"

"Oh, I don't know," replied the second goat. "I thought the book was better."

*   *   *

A man's car stalled on a country road. When he got out to fix it, a cow came along and stopped beside him. "Your trouble is probably in the carburetor," said the cow.

Startled, the man jumped back and ran down the road until he met a farmer. He told the farmer his story.

"Was it a large red cow with a brown spot over the right eye?" asked the farmer.

"Yes, yes," the man replied.

"Oh! I wouldn't listen to Bessie," said the farmer.

"She doesn't know anything about cars."

*   *   *

Etiquette is learning to yawn with your mouth shut.

*   *   *

"Did you fall down the elevator shaft?"
"No, I was sitting here and they built it around me."

*   *   *

Lady: You should be ashamed to ask for handouts in this neighborhood.
Tramp: Don't apologize for it, ma'am. I've seen worse.

*   *   *

"Tell me the story about the girl that bleached her hair."
"I never tell off-color stories."

*   *   *

Three out of four things you worry about happening don't happen; and three out of four things you don't worry about happening do. Which all goes to prove that even if you're worrying about the wrong things, you're doing just about the right amount of worrying!

*   *   *

I was reading one of those "Previews of 1980" articles and they claim by 1980 they'll be able to heat

an entire apartment building with one lump of coal!
By 1980? I've got a landlord who's trying to do it
now!

*　　*　　*

Some of these teenage singing groups ... they
look like they've cut more throats than records.

*　　*　　*

I guess you read about the rock and rool show that
turned into a riot. What bothers me is, how could
they tell?

*　　*　　*

Did you hear about the man who jumped from the
Empire State Building and lived to tell about it? He
told the people on the 93rd floor, those on the 84th
floor, everyone on the 62nd floor, and those on ...

*　　*　　*

City Slicker: Look at that bunch of cows.
Farmer: Not bunch ... herd?
City Slicker: Heard what?
Farmer: Herd of cows.
City Slicker: Sure, I've heard of cows.
Farmer: No, a cow herd.
City Slicker: Why should I care what a cow heard?
I've got no secrets from a cow.

*　　*　　*

Always borrow from a pessimist ... he never ex-
pects it back anyhow.

*　　*　　*

Last month I was in California. Stopped at one of the best hotels. To give you an idea of how big my room was, when I closed the door, the doorknob got in bed with me.

I said to the clerk, "Give me another room."

He gave me another key. I put the key in the keyhole and broke the window.

*   *   *

"I heard about an artist who painted a cobweb on the ceiling so realistically that the maid spent hours trying to get it down."

"Sorry, I don't believe it."

"Why not? Artists have been known to do such things."

"Yes, but maids haven't."

*   *   *

"Can you keep a secret?"

"Sure."

"I need to borrow some money."

"Don't worry. It's just as if I never heard it."

*   *   *

Fred: There is a man outside with a wooden leg named Martin.

Jed: What is the name of his other leg?

*   *   *

I love Christmas. I receive a lot of wonderful presents I can't wait to exchange.

*   *   *

One time when my friend was in the breeding

business, he crossed a parrot with a tiger. He doesn't know what it is, but when it talks, everybody listens.

* * *

Don't knock the weather. Nine-tenths of the people couldn't start a conversation if it didn't change once in a while.

* * *

Nowadays, whatever is not worth saying is sung.

* * *

"Have you ever had your ears pierced?"
"No, but I have often had them bored."

* * *

A pessimist is one who when faced with two evils chooses them both.

* * *

Did you hear about the Texan who was trying to make a phone call?

"Operator, how much does it cost to call New York?"

"Three dollars and seventy-five cents," replied the operator.

"Why, I can call Hell and back for that much," said the Texan.

"Yes, sir," said the operator, "that's a local call!"

* * *

"My poor fellow," said the lady, "here is a quarter for you. It must be dreadful to be lame, but just think how much worse it would be if you were blind."

"Yer right, lady," agreed the beggar. "When I was blind I was always getting counterfeit money."

* * *

"I gave the man thirty cents for saving my life."
"What did he do?"
"He gave me twenty-five cents in change."

* * *

"When your dog howls all night it is a sign of death."
"Whose, I wonder?"
"Your dog's, if he howls again tonight!"

* * *

"I drink fifty cups of coffee a day."
"Doesn't that keep you awake?"
"It helps."

* * *

Unions are getting such a bad name, it's no wonder they're called Brother Hoods.

* * *

Ozark Proverb: Terrible is the fate to have a rooster who is silent and a hen who crows.

* * *

A slanderer is a guy who says things behind your back he wouldn't say to your face.

A flatterer is a guy who says things to your face he wouldn't say behind your back.

*　　*　　*

A Californian was visiting his Texan cousin and while walking with the cousin across a barren section of land, saw a funny looking bird flop across the road in front of them. "What is it?" the Californian asked.

"It's a bird of paradise," replied his Texan cousin.

The Californian replied, "Long way from home, isn't he?"

*　　*　　*

We live in the Metal Age:
   Silver in the hair.
   Gold in the teeth.
   Lead in the pants.
   Iron in the veins.

*　　*　　*

Actor: As a matter of fact, I have received letters from ladies in almost every place in which I have appeared.

Rival: Landladies, I presume.

*　　*　　*

1st Gossip: She told me that you told her the secret I told you not to tell her.

2nd Gossip: The mean thing! I told her not to tell you I told her.

1st Gossip: Well, don't tell her that I told you she told me.

*　　*　　*

At a reception in Washington, a young man was asked by a widow to guess her age. "You must have some idea," she said, as he hesitated.

"I have several ideas," he admitted, with a smile. "The trouble is that I hesitate whether to make it ten years younger on account of your looks or ten years older on account of your intelligence.

*　　*　　*

The man of the house finally took all the disabled umbrellas to the repairer's. Two days later, on his way to his office, when he got up to leave the streetcar, he absent-mindedly laid hold of the umbrella belonging to a woman beside him. The woman cried, "Stop thief!" rescued her umbrella and covered the man with shame and confusion.

The same day, he stopped at the repairer's and received all eight of his umbrellas duly repaired. As he entered a streetcar, with the unwrapped umbrellas tucked under his arm, he was horrified to behold glaring at him the lady of his morning adventure. Her voice came to him charged with withering scorn: "Huh! Had a good day, didn't you!"

*　　*　　*

Did you hear about the new tooth paste that has shoe polish in it? It is for people who put their foot in their mouth.

*　　*　　*

One word of advice . . . don't give it.

*　　*　　*

I enjoy just visiting my friends so I can look at my library and all my garden tools.

*　　*　　*

"Do you file your nails?"

"No, I just cut them off and throw them away."

* * *

A little prospector wearing clean new shoes waked into a saloon. A big Texan said to his friend standing at the bar, "Watch me make this dude dance." He walked over to the prospector and said, "You're a foreigner, aren't you? From the East?"

"You might say that," the little prospector answered. "I'm from Boston and I'm here prospecting for gold."

"Now tell me something. Can you dance?"

"No, sir. I never did learn to dance."

"Well, I'm going to teach you. You'll be surprised how quickly you can learn."

With that, the Texan took out his gun and started shooting at the prospector's feet. Hopping, skipping, jumping, by the time the little prospector made it to the door he was shaking like a leaf.

About an hour later the Texan left the saloon. As soon as he stepped outside the door, he heard a click. He looked around and there, four feet from his head, was the biggest shotgun he had ever seen.

And the little prospector said, "Mr. Texan, have you ever kissed a mule?"

"No," said the quick thinking Texan, "but I've always wanted to."

* * *

A lady visited a crystal gazer and was shocked to learn that her fee was twenty-five dollars, which, stated the seer, "entitles you to ask me two questions."

"Isn't that a lot of money for only two questions?" demanded the lady.

"Yes, madam, it is," replied the fortune teller. "And now what is your second question?"

"Have I asked one?"

"Yes, and that's the second!"

*　　*　　*

The five "B's" of old age are:

Bifocals . . . bunions . . . bridges . . . bulges . . . and baldness.

*　　*　　*

"Say, Mr. Farmer, we helped ourselves to some of your apples."

"That's okay. I helped myself to some of the tools in your car while you were in the orchard."

*　　*　　*

What is irritating about love is that it is a crime that requires an accomplice.

*　　*　　*

The latest thing for a man who has everything is a calendar to remind him when the payments are due.

*　　*　　*

Did you hear about the egg in the monastery? Out of the frying pan, into the friar.

*　　*　　*

"Twenty years from now," said a poor writer who was having trouble with his landlord, "people will come by and look at this house and say, 'Phillips, the famous writer, had a room here.' "

The landlord was unimpressed. "Phillips, I'm telling you that if you don't pay your rent, they'll be saying that day after tomorrow!"

* * *

Immigration men are knowledgeable. They are pretty clever guys. This one fellow in particular has a little trick. He asks: "What's your nationality?" "American." "American, huh? Do you know the words of the Star Spangled Banner?" "No, I don't." "You're an American, go in."

* * *

"Why do you think you have so many friends?"
"I guess it is because I always play my tuba when I am lonely."

* * *

"I had a terrible dream. I dreamed I was marooned on an island with twelve beautiful women."
"What's wrong with that?"
"Did you ever try and cook and wash for twelve women?"

* * *

"Did you hear the story about the window you couldn't see through?"
"No."
"Well, that's okay . . . it's too dirty to tell anyway!"

* * *

"All the kids at school say I look like a monkey."
"Hush up and comb your face!"

* * *

"Did the movie have a happy ending?"
"Yes, everyone was glad it was over."

* * *

A man was sitting in a cafe when all of a sudden someone came in and beat him up. When he woke up he said to the owner: "Who was that?" "That was Kung Fu from China," replied the owner.

Next week the man was eating in the same cafe when a different person entered and beat him up. When he woke up he said to the owner: "Who was that?" The owner said, "That was Kuang Chow from Taiwan."

Several weeks later Kung Fu and Kuang Chow were eating in the cafe. The man who had been beaten by both of them entered and did his work. He said to the owner, "When they wake, tell them that that was 'a hammer from Sears.'"

* * *

Did you hear about one of the Women's Lip (Oh, I mean Women's Lib) Movement leaders who said, "Girls, one day we will have women in the Mayor's office, in the Governor's office, in Congress and one day a woman will be President of the United States. And, along the way, if the going gets tough, you can always pray to God and she will hear you."

* * *

I learned how to swim the old way when I was about five years old. My Dad took me out to the middle of a lake in a boat and then threw me in the water. The swim back to shore was not too bad . . . it was getting out of the gunny sack.

*   *   *

I heard so much about the bad effects of marijuana I'm afraid to eat pot roast.

*   *   *

Joe: Why do you keep scratching yourself?
Moe: I'm the only one who knows where it itches.

*   *   *

I went to a rock festival last summer and it was fascinating. There were four hundred girls, five hundred boys and fifty uncommitted.

*   *   *

Remember this before you burden other people with your troubles. Half of them aren't the least bit interested, and the rest are delighted that you're getting what they think is coming to you.

*   *   *

Once upon a time there was a parrot who could say only three little words: "Who is it?" One day when the parrot was alone in the house, there was a loud knock on the door. "Who is it?" screeched the parrot. "It's the plumber," the visitor responded. "Who is it?" repeated the parrot. "It's the plumber, I tell you," was the reply. "You called me to tell me your cellar was flooded." Again the parrot called, "Who is it?" By this time, the plumber became so angry that he fainted. A neighbor rushed over to see the cause of the commotion and found the visitor who had died because of a heart attack. He looked at the man and said, "Who is it?" The parrot answered, "It's the plumber!"

* * *

"Dear me," said the old lady on a visit to the mountains, "look at all those rocks. Where did they call come from?"

"The glaciers brought them down," said the guide.

"But where are the glaciers?"

"The glaciers," said the guide with a weary voice, "have gone back for more rocks."

* * *

A guy walked up to me in Hollywood and said, "Psst, buddy! Wanna see a clean movie?"

* * *

I'm not a liar, sir. I just remember big!

* * *

Most of us have two chances of becoming wealthy . . . slim and none.

* * *

Daniel Webster was once bested by one of the farmers of his native state. He had been hunting at some distance from his inn, and rather than make the long trip back, he approached a farmhouse some considerable time after dark and pounded on the door. An upstairs window was raised and the farmer, with head thrust out, called, "What do you want?"

"I want to spend the night here," said Webster.

"All right. Stay there," said the farmer. Down went the window.

*   *   *

Talk about bad situations . . . just think about:

A screen door on a submarine.
A stowaway on a kamikaze plane.
A teenager who parks in a dark alley with his girl
    and his horn gets stuck.
A soup sandwich.
One who ejects from a helicopter.
A Hindu snake charmer with a deaf cobra.

*   *   *

A bookseller had a statement for a book curtly returned to him with this note written across it: "Dear Sir: I never ordered this beastly book. If I did, you didn't sent it. If you sent it, I never got it. If I got it, I paid for it. If I didn't, I won't!"

*   *   *

"I think I labor too hard sometimes. I'm a farmer and I work fifteen hours a day, seven days a week."
    "What do you grow?"
    "Very tired."

*   *   *

When a skyscraper's elevator broke down, one passenger raced down twenty-two floors of spiral stairways so fast he drilled himself into the basement.

*   *   *

I have been having some trouble with the new car I

bought. I added a carburetor that saved 30% on gas, a timer that saved 50% on gas, and spark plugs that saved 30% on gas. I drove 10 miles and the gas tank overflowed.

* * *

A Texan was trying to impress on a Bostonian the valor of the heroes of the Alamo. "I'll bet you never had anything so brave around Boston," said the Texan.

"Did you hear of Paul Revere?" asked the Bostonian.

"Paul Revere?" said the Texan. "Isn't he the guy who ran for help?"

* * *

"According to this report a man gets hit by an automobile every twenty minutes."

"What a glutton for punishment that guy is."

* * *

My seat belt makes me drive safely. I sit on it and the buckle keeps me awake.

* * *

I went for a ride with a friend of mine that has a new car with all the latest safety devices. When I got out of the car, I unbuckled the seat belt, unbuckled the safety belt, unbuckled the shoulder belt . . . all the belts. I stepped out of the car and my pants fell down!

* * *

This afternoon I saw two little cars under a station

wagon. I didn't know if they were hiding or nursing.

*   *   *

"I know about a motorist, going eighty, who tried to beat a speeding train to an intersection."

"Did the motorist get across?"

"He got a cross, all right . . . a beautiful marble cross purchased by his beneficiaries."

*   *   *

Alaskan cities are growing so fast, they're beginning to have traffic problems. Just last week, Dawson City put up its first traffic signal. It says: MUSH . . . DON'T MUSH!

*   *   *

A man returned to his sports car to find a freshly crushed fender and this note affixed to his windshield wiper: "The people who saw me sideswipe your fender are now watching me write this note, and doubtless figure I'm tell you my name and address so you can contact me and send me the bill. Ho! Ho! You should live so long."

*   *   *

An old gent was passing a busy intersection when a large St. Bernard brushed against him and knocked him down. An instant later a foreign sports car skidded around the corner and inflicted more damage.

A bystander helped him up and asked him if the dog had hurt him. "Well," he answered, "the dog didn't hurt so much, but that tin can tied to his tail nearly killed me."

*   *   *

"I hate vague, non-committal and middle-of-the-road people, don't you?

"Mmmmmmmmmm!"

*   *   *

ON THE JOB

"Your methods of farming are out of date," said an agricultural student to an old farmer. "I'd be surprised if you got eight pounds of oranges off of that tree."

"So would I," said the old farmer. "That is a pear tree."

*   *   *

"What happened to the other barber that used to be here?"

"Well, he is now in the home for the insane. His business was slow and one day he asked a customer if he wanted a shampoo and the customer said, 'No.' I guess that was the last straw. He took a razor and slashed the customer's throat. By the way, how about a shampoo today?"

"Sure, go ahead," said the customer.

*   *   *

"It was a terrible day at the office, dear. The computer stopped and we all had to think."

*   *   *

Traveler: What does this pigsty cost?

Innkeeper: For one pig, $5.00; for two pigs, $9.00.

*   *   *

A traveling salesman was held up in the West by a storm and flood. He wired his office in New York: DELAYED BY STORM. SEND INSTRUCTIONS.

His boss wired back: COMMENCE VACATION IMMEDIATELY.

*   *   *

Business was pretty bad at Max's Bargain Emporium. Then, to compound his troubles, Harry's on his right decided to run a big Going Out Of Business Sale and hung up a sign reading: THE GREATEST GOING OUT OF BUSINESS SALE EVER. YOU COULDN'T GET BIGGER BARGAINS IF WE WERE REALLY GOING OUTBUSINESS.

Then Leo, on Max's left, decided to run a sale and hung up a sign reading: FIRE SALE. YOU COULDN'T GET BETTER BUYS EVEN IF THERE WAS A REAL FIRE.

Max joined the fun. He hung up a sign directly between the others reading: ENTRANCE TO SALE.

*   *   *

Carpenter: You hammer like lightning.
Apprentice: Really fast, huh?
Carpenter: No . . . you seldom hit the same place twice.

*   *   *

"How many make a dozen?"
"Twelve."
"And how many make a million?"
"Very few."

*   *   *

A passerby stopped and said, "You're diggin' out some holes, I see."

"No, sir," was the reply. "I'm diggin' out the dirt an' leavin' the holes."

*   *   *

Employee: Sir, my wife . . . er . . . told me I must ask for an increase.

Employer: Well, I'll ask my wife if I can give you one.

*   *   *

Wife: I've been asked for a reference for our last maid. I've said she's lazy, unpunctual and impertinent. How can I add anything in her favor?

Husband: You might say that she's got a good appetite and sleeps well.

*   *   *

A quack was selling an elixir which he declared would make men live to a great age.

"Look at me," he shouted. "Hale and hearty. I'm over 300 years old."

"Is he really as old as that?" asked a listener of the youthful assistant.

"I can't say," replied the assistant. "I've only worked for him for 97 years.

*   *   *

Through an error, an employee took home a blank check in his pay envelope. When he opened it up he said, "Just as I thought. My deductions have finally caught up with my salary."

*   *   *

Barber to a customer with a lot of grease on his hair: "Do you want it cut or just an oil change?"

*　　*　　*

Have you heard about the new electric car that runs on $2.50 worth of power a month? One slight catch . . . the extension cord costs $12,000.

*　　*　　*

"My barber specializes in road map shaves."
"What is that?"
"When he finishes, your face is full of short cuts."

*　　*　　*

1st employee: How long have you been working here?
2nd employee: Ever since the day the foreman threatened to fire me.

*　　*　　*

"I hear that Detroit is coming out with a pollution-free car next year."
"Cleaner engine?"
"No, tighter windows."

*　　*　　*

Sign for pantyhose: "Long Janes"

*　　*　　*

A committee is a group of the unprepared, appointed by the unwilling, to the unnecessary.

*　　*　　*

In the window of a hearing aid shop: "Trust us. Over 5,000 ears of experience."

* * *

A man had ridden three miles in a taxi when he suddenly realized he had left his wallet at home. He leaned forward and told the driver: "Stop at the drugstore for a minute. I want to get some matches so I can look for a $20 bill I've lost back here."

When he came out of the drugstore, the taxi had disappeared.

* * *

By working faithfully eight hours a day, you may eventually get to be a boss and work twelve hours a day.

* * *

Some people are like blisters. They don't show up until the work is finished.

* * *

Employment manager: It looks to me as if you've been fired from every job you ever had!

Applicant: Well, you've got to admit I'm no quitter.

* * *

Salesman: If you buy this home freezer you could save enough on food bills to pay for it.

Housewife: But we are buying a car on the bus fare we save, paying for the washer on laundry bills we save, and paying for the house on rent we save. We just can't afford to save any more right now.

*   *   *

1st Salesman: I've made some valuable contacts today.

2nd Salesman: I didn't make any sales, either.

*   *   *

Employee: Say, boss, your assistant just died, and I was wondering if I could take his place?

Boss: It's all right with me if you can arrange it with the undertaker!

*   *   *

Employee: Could I have a raise? (Shaking a little)

Manager: You can't come in here like this and ask for a raise. You have only been with the company two weeks. You have to work yourself up first.

Employee: But I did . . . look . . . I'm trembling all over!

*   *   *

"I am planning a salary increase for you, young man."

"When does it become effective?"

"Just as soon as you do!"

*   *   *

Going out of business has become so profitable for one merchant that he's opening a chain of going-out-of-business stores.

*   *   *

Small car salesman to prospect: "It only seats two but can easily accommodate 14 bumper stickers."

*   *   *

Visitor: How many people work here in your plant?

Manager: Oh, about one out of ten!

*   *   *

"Miss Hatfield, I was just reading over this letter you did. Your typing is really improving. I see there are only seven mistakes here."

"Thank you, sir."

"Now, let's take a look at the second line."

*   *   *

Employer: How's your spelling? Let me hear you spell Mississippi.

Secretary: The river or the state?

*   *   *

Politician: What we need is a working majority.

Merchant: What we really need is a majority working.

*   *   *

A young man came for an interview with a bank president.

"Tell me, sir, how did you become so successful?"

"Two words."

"And what are they, sir?"

"Right decisions."

"How do you make right decisions?"

"One word . . . experience."

"And how do you get experience?"

"Two words."

"And what are they?"

"Wrong decisions!"

*　　*　　*

"Here's one name on the committee that I never heard of."

"Oh, that's probably the person who actually does the work."

*　　*　　*

An antique collector, passing through a small village, stopped to watch an old man chopping wood with an ancient ax.

"That's a mighty old ax you have there," remarked the collector.

"Yes," said the villager, "it once belonged to George Washington."

"Not really!" gasped the collector. "It's certainly stood up well."

"Of course," admitted the old man, "it's had three new handles and two new heads."

*　　*　　*

Jones came into the office an hour late for the third time in one week and found the boss waiting for him. "What's the story this time, Jones?" he asked sarcastically. "Let's hear a good excuse for a change." Jones sighed, "Everything went wrong this morning, boss. The wife decided to drive me to the station. She got ready in ten minutes, but then the drawbridge got stuck. Rather than let you down, I swam across the river (look, my suit's still damp), ran out to the airport, got a ride on Mr. Thompson's helicopter, landed on top of Radio City Music Hall, and was carried here piggy-back by one of the Rockettes." "You'll have to do better than that, Jones," said the boss, obviously disappointed. "No woman can get ready in ten minutes."

*   *   *

One day an employee arrived late with one eye closed, his left arm in a sling, and his clothes in tatters. "It's nine-thirty," pointed out the president, "and you were due at eight-thirty." The employee explained, "I fell out of a tenth-story window." The president snorted, "It took you a whole hour?"

*   *   *

Note inside of pay enevelope: EMPLOYEES SHOULD NOT DISCUSS THEIR SALARIES WITH OTHERS.

The employee said, "Don't worry! I'm as ashamed of it as you are."

*   *   *

"I used to be a pilot in a stable."

"That's ridiculous."

"Really, I was a pilot in a stable. I used to pilot here, pilot there . . .

*   *   *

Butcher: I was wondering if you'd like to buy a henway. There's a special on them today.

Customer: What's a henway?

Butcher: Oh, about four or five pounds.

*   *   *

"My brother is working with five thousand men under him."

"Where?"

"Mowing lawns in a cemetery."

*   *   *

Stranger: I've come out here to make a honest living.

Native: Well, there's not much competition.

*   *   *

Two truck drivers applied for a job. One said, "I'm Pete and this is my partner Mike; when I drive at night, he sleeps.

The man said, "All right, I'll give you an oral test. It's three o'clock in the morning. You're on a little bridge and your truck is loaded with nitroglycerin. All of a sudden a truck comes toward you at about eighty miles per hour. What's the first thing you do?"

"I wake up my partner Mike . . . He never saw a wreck like this before."

*   *   *

The customer wanted to buy a chicken and the butcher had only one in stock. He weighed it and said, "A beauty. That will be $1.25, lady."

"Oh, that's not quite large enough," said the customer. The butcher put the chicken back in the refrigerator, rolled it around on the ice several times, then back on the scales again.

"This one is $1.85," he said, adding his thumb for good weight.

"Oh, that' fine!" said the customer. "I'll take both of them."

*   *   *

Motorist: What will it cost to fix my car?
Mechanic: What's wrong with it?
Motorist: I don't know?
Mechanic: $79.95!

*   *   *

1st Steno: We call Mr. Jones the office locomotive.

2nd Steno: Why? Because he does so much work?

1st Steno: No, because all he does is run back and forth, smoke and whistle.

*　　*　　*

There's a story going the rounds that involves a carpet layer who had worked all day installing wall-to-wall carpeting. When he noticed a lump under the carpet in the middle of the living room, he felt his shirt pocket for his cigarettes—they were gone. He was not about to take up the carpet, so he went outside for a two-by-four. Tamping down cigarettes with it would be easy. Once the lump was smoothed, the man gathered up his tools and carried them to the truck. Then two things happened simultaneously. He saw his cigarettes on the seat of the truck, and over his shoulder he heard the voice of the woman to whom the carpet belonged. "Have you seen anything of my parakeet?" she asked plaintively.

*　　*　　*

"Now this is the verbal part of your employment test. What does Aurora Borealis mean?"

"It means I don't get the job!"

*　　*　　*

Employer: Look here! What did you mean by telling me you had five year's experience when you've never even had a job before!

Man: Well, you advertized for a man with imagination!

*　　*　　*

Customer: How much are your eggs?

Storeowner: Sixty cents a dozen and thirty cents if they're cracked.

Customer: Well, then, crack me a dozen!

*   *   *

A big executive boarded a New York to Chicago train. He explained to the porter: "I'm a heavy sleeper and I want you to be sure and wake me at 3:00 a.m. to get off in Buffalo. Regardless of what I say, get me up, for I have some important business there."

The next morning he awakened in Chicago. He found the porter and really poured it on with abusive language.

After he had left, someone said, "How could you stand there and take that kind of talk from that man?"

The porter said: "That ain't nothing. You should have heard what the man said that I put off in Buffalo."

*   *   *

"How did you become such a successful door-to-door salesman?"

"Because of the first five words I would utter when a woman would open the door. 'Miss, is your mother in?' "

*   *   *

"That horse you sold me is almost blind."

"Well, I told you he was a fine horse but that he didn't look good."

*   *   *

I bought a suit that comes from London. It was

87

brought here and sold to a wholesaler. The wholesaler sold it to a retailer and the retailer sold it to me. To think all those people are making a living out of something I haven't paid for yet.

* * *

So this druggist is filling a prescription, hands his customer a little bottle with 12 pills in it, and says, "That'll be $4.50." Suddenly the phone rings and as the druggist turns to answer it, the customer puts 50¢ on the counter, walks out. The druggist turns back, spots the 50¢ and yells: "Sir! Sir! That's $4.50 not 50¢. Sir!" The guy is gone. The druggist picks up the half a buck, looks at it, shrugs, flips it into the till and mumbles: "Oh, well, 40¢ profit is better than nothing."

* * *

You'll have to excuse me but I'm going through a very difficult time in a man's life. I'm too tired to work and too broke to quit.

* * *

Customer: I'm sorry, but I won't be able to pay for this suit for two months.
Tailor: Oh, that's all right.
Customer: When will it be ready?
Tailor: In two months.

* * *

Milkman: Are you sure you want 54 quarts of milk?
Lady: Yes. My doctor told me to take a bath in milk.

Milkman: Do you want it pasteurized?
Lady: No, just up to my chin.

*   *   *

"Were you hired by the radio station?"
"N-n-no, they s-s-said I w-w-wasn't t-t-tall enough!"

*   *   *

I just found out why I feel tired all the time.

We made a survey and found I was doing more than my share of the world's work.

The population of the country is 160 million, but there are 62 million over 60 years of age. That leaves 98 million to do the work. People under 21 years of age total 54 million which leaves 44 million to do the work.

Then there are 21 million who are employed by the government and that leaves 23 million to do the work. Ten million are in the Armed Forces. That leaves 13 million to do the work. Now deduct 12,800,000, the number in state and city offices and that leaves 200,000 to do the work. There are 126,000 in hospitals, insane asylums and so forth, and that leaves 74,000 people to do the work.

But 62,000 of these refuse to work, so that leaves 12,000 to do the work. Now it may interest you to know that there are 11,988 people in jail, so that leaves just TWO people to do all the work and that's YOU and ME and I'm getting tired doing everything myself.

*   *   *

SMOGARIAN ARISE

Q. Do you know what the happiest day in a Smogarian's life was?

A. When he found out he could put Right Guard under his left arm.

* * *

Did you hear about the Smogarian who was going to have his head cut off? They put him on the block and pulled the trip cord. The blade came part way down and stopped. The Smogarian was heard to say, "If you would oil that pully, I think it would work better."

* * *

Did you hear about the sad case of the Smogarian actor who fell off a ship passing a lighthouse. He drowned swimming in circles. He was trying to keep in the spotlight.

* * *

Did you hear about the Smogarian who found some milk bottles in the grass? He thought that he had found a cow's nest.

* * *

An overheard conversation in the Smogarian Rocket Center: "Why did our first moon rocket miss by 27,000 miles?

"I think," said a Smogarian rocket scientist, "that 84,217 Smogarians jumped on the seesaw bouncer one eight of a second too soon."

*   *   *

Q. Why do the Smogarians have three men in their police patrols?

A. Because the first policeman can read but not write, and the second can write but not read. The third is a faithful party man put there to keep an eye on the intellectuals.

*   *   *

Did you hear about the Smogarian who won a Gold Metal in the Olympics? He took it home and had it bronzed.

*   *   *

Did you hear about the Smogarians who hijacked a submarine? They asked for $250,000 and three parachutes.

*   *   *

Q. Do you know how to make a Smogarian's nose 8 inches long?

A. Fold it in half.

*   *   *

Did you hear about the Smogarian that planted light bulbs in his garden? He heard that tulips grew from bulbs.

*   *   *

Q. Do you know how many gears there are on a Smogarian tank?

A. Five. Four in reverse and one forward. The one forward is in case they get attacked from the rear.

*　　　*　　　*

Q. Do you know who put the last 10 bullets into Mussolini's body?

A. 10,000 Smogarian sharpshooters.

*　　　*　　　*

Did you hear about the two Smogarians who got married in a bathtub? It was a double ring ceremony.

*　　　*　　　*

Did you hear about the Smogarian who bet $10 on a football game and lost? He bet $10 more on the instant replay and lost again.

*　　　*　　　*

Someone told the Smogarians that they could not send a rocket to the sun because it would burn up. They said that it would be all right because they were going to travel at night.

*　　　*　　　*

Q. Why do Smogarians have big noses?

A. Air is free.

*　　　*　　　*

Q. Do you know what the favorite underarm spray deodorant of Smogaria is?

A. Raid.

*　　　*　　　*

Did you hear about the merchant that had a contest and offered one week's vacation in Smogaria as first prize; and for the second prize, two week's vacation in Smogaria?

*　　*　　*

Q. Do you know how to tell the difference between a Smogarian funeral and a wedding?
A. One less drunk.

*　　*　　*

Did you hear about the Smogarian elevator operator that got fired? He forgot the route.

*　　*　　*

Did you hear about the Smogarian who had a pig under his arm? Someone asked, "Where did you get that?" The pig replied, "I won him at the fair."

*　　*　　*

Did you hear about the Smogarian problem of evolution? From ape to man . . . only they didn't jump far enough.

*　　*　　*

Did you hear about 10 Smogarians that drowned? They tried to hijack a train to Cuba.

*　　*　　*

Q. Do you know why they do not let Smogarians swim in the ocean?
A. It causes rings on the pier.

*　　*　　*

Man: Did you hear that joke about the Egyptian guide who showed some tourists two skulls of Cleopatra, one as a girl and one as a woman?
Smogarian: No, let's hear it.

* * *

Q. Do you know who the intelligence officer for Smogaria was during the Second World War?
A. Nobody.

* * *

Did you hear about the Smogarian fish that drowned?

* * *

Did you hear that the Smogarians just invented an ejection seat for a helicopter?

* * *

Q. Do you know why Smogarians have big noses?
A. They have big fingers.

* * *

Q. Do you know who has an I.Q. of 180?
A. Smogaria.

* * *

Q. Do you know how the Smogarians got to America?
A. Two swam across and the rest walked over on the dead fish.

* * *

Q. Do you know how many pallbearers there are at a Smogarian funeral?

A. Two. There are only two handles on a garbage can.

*   *   *

Q. How can you tell a Smogarian funeral?

A. All the garbage trucks have their lights on.

*   *   *

Q. Do you know how to sink a Smogarian battleship?

A. Put it in the water.

*   *   *

Q. What is the easiest job in Smogaria?

A. Filling out the intelligence test.

*   *   *

An Austrian, an Italian, and a Smogarian all applied for the same job. The job called for someone to tend one thousand sheep halfway up a high mountain. The rancher couldn't decide which one to hire, so he sent all three up to have a go.

The second day, the Austrian came down; he couldn't stand the smell. The third day, the Italian came down, he couldn't stand the smell. The fourth day, the one thousand sheep came down.

*   *   *

Q. Why do Smogarians have broad shoulders?

A. They rat the hair under their arms.

*   *   *

Q. What do they call it when 10 Smogarians jump out of an airplane?
A. Air pollution.

* * *

Q. What group stands in a circle and points guns at each other?
A. A Smogarian firing squad.

* * *

Did you hear about the Smogarian who bought snow tires? They melted the next day.

* * *

Did you hear about the Smogarian who got killed by a cow? It fell on him while he was getting a drink.

* * *

Did you hear about the Smogarian parachute that opens upon the point of impact?

* * *

Do you know what happened when an atom bomb fell on Smogaria? It caused about $1.15 in damages.

* * *

POLITICS AND TAXES

A politician was giving a speech in a rural district when a yokel tossed a cabbage onto the platform.

The quick thinking politician gave it a sidelong glance and said, "It appears that one of my opponents has lost his head."

* * *

"What would be a good way to raise revenue and still benefit the people?"
"Tax every political speech."

* * *

Money talks . . . It says goodbye.

* * *

Political orator: Yes, I have heard the voice of the people calling me to duty.
Heckler: Maybe it was an echo.

* * *

"Well, election time will soon be here. I plan to run for office again. I guess the air will soon be full of my speeches."
"Yeah! . . . and vice versa!"

* * *

"My father was a great Western politician in his day."
"Yeah? What did he run for?"
"The border."

* * *

Political orator: All that I am or will be, I owe to my mother. Heckler: Why don't you send her 30¢ and square the account?

*   *   *

Tax collector: Why don't you pay your taxes with a smile?

Taxpayer: I'd love to but you insist on money!

*   *   *

Conscience is that still small voice that tells you the Internal Revenue Service might check your return.

*   *   *

The cost of living is going up and the chance of living is going down.

*   *   *

When I was a boy, I was told anybody could become president. I'm now beginning to believe it!

*   *   *

Inflation: That's when something you bought for $5 a few years ago costs $10 to repair.

*   *   *

Inflation hasn't ruined everything. A dime still can be used as a screwdriver.

*   *   *

An important politician called to visit a friend at an insane asylum and while there tried to phone his office. But his connection was constantly delayed, and in exasperation he said to the operator: "Young lady, do you know who I am?"

"No," she replied. "But I know where you are."

A distraught taxpayer handed in his income tax return with his check to the Internal Revenue agent.

"Boy," complained the man, "the boys in Washington are a heartless bunch. They sure cleaned out my bank account!"

"Cheer up," consoled the revenue man. "Remember what Benjamin Franklin said: 'Nothing is certain but death and taxes.' "

"Yeah," said the taxpayer, "I only wish they came in that order."

*   *   *

I'm a little worried about this year's income tax. I think I made it out wrong. I've got 42¢ left.

*   *   *

It's Election Day in a small Russian village and all the citizens are lined up in front of City Hall. Each is handed a sealed envelope and told to drop it into the ballot box. One peasant takes the envelope and tears it open. Immediately he's surrounded by outraged officials yelling: "Comrade! Comrade! What are you doing? Don't you realize this is a secret ballot?"

*   *   *

I understand (use appropriate town or city) is having financial problems. I have the answer. We secede from the Union; form a new country; then we apply to the United States for foreign aid!

*   *   *

Today, with all this inflation going on, about all

you can get for a dollar is a picture of George Washington.

*   *   *

"Do you like conceited politicians as much as the other kind?"
"What other kind?"

*   *   *

After a political rally, a wife came home late and sank into a chair. "Everything is going great. We are going to sweep the country."
To which her husband responded, "Why not start with the living room?"

*   *   *

Pity poor old George Washington. He couldn't blame his troubles on the previous administration.

*   *   *

Americans are getting stronger. Twenty years ago it took two people to carry ten dollars worth of groceries. Today, a five-year-old does it.

*   *   *

A man walked up to a farmer as he came out of a voting booth, "I'm from the FBI." "What seems to be the trouble?" "We happen to know that you accepted a bribe and sold your vote." "That's not true. I voted for the candidate because I like him." "Well, that's where we've got you. We have concrete evidence you accepted fifty dollars from him." "Well, it's plain common sense, if someone gives you fifty dollars, you're going to like him."

*   *   *

A diplomat is one who thinks twice before saying nothing.

*   *   *

I don't know if we'll ever get a cure for poverty, but the way taxes and prices are going up, we've got a sure cure for wealth!

*   *   *

Who Pays The Bill

In reply to your request to send a check, I wish to inform you that the present condition of my bank account makes it almost impossible.

My shattered financial conditions are due to Federal laws, corporation laws, mothers-in-law, brothers-in-law, sisters-in-law, and outlaws.

Through these taxes I am compelled to pay a business tax, assessment tax, head tax, school tax, income tax, casket tax, food tax, furniture tax, sales tax and excise tax. Even my brain is taxed.

I am required to get a business license, car license, hunting license, fishing license, truck and auto license, not to mention marriage and dog license. I am also required to contribute to every society and organization which the genius of man is capable of bringing into life; to women's relief, unemployed relief, and gold digger's relief. Also to every hospital and charitable institution in the city, including the Red Cross, the Black Cross, the Purple Cross and the Double Cross.

For my own safety, I am compelled to carry life insurance, liability insurance, burglary insurance, accident insurance, property insurance, business insurance, earthquake insurance, tornado insurance, unemployment insurance, old age insurance and fire insurance.

My own business is so governed that it is no easy matter for me to find out who owns it. I am inspected, suspected, disrespected, rejected, dejected, and compelled until I prove an inexhaustible supply of money for every known need of the human race.

Simply because I refuse to donate something or another I am boycotted, talked about, lied about, held up, held down and robbed until I am almost ruined. I can tell you honestly that except for a miracle that happened I could not enclose this check. The wolf that comes to my door nowadays just had pups in my kitchen. I sold them and here's the money.

Would like more business to pay more taxes.

Sincerely yours,

*   *   *

Medicare

A sample of what might happen if we had socialized medicine is currently making the rounds. It goes something like this:

A man feeling the need of medical care went to the medical building for that purpose, and upon entering the front door found himself faced with a battery of doors, each marked with the names of ailments such as appendicitis, heart, cancer, etc.

He felt sure his trouble could be diagnosed as appendicitis, so he entered the door so marked. Upon entering, he found himself faced with two more doors, one marked male and the other female. He entered the door marked male and found himself in another corridor where there were two doors, one marked Protestant and the other Catholic.

Since he was a Protestant, he entered the proper door and found himself facing two more doors, one marked white and the other colored. He entered the white door and again was faced with two more doors marked taxpayer and nontaxpayer. He still owned equity in his home, so he went through the door marked taxpayer, and found himself confronted with two more doors marked single and married.

He had a wife at home, so he entered the proper door and once more there were two more doors, one marked Republican and the other Democrat.

SINCE HE WAS A REPUBLICAN HE ENTERED THE DOOR AND FELL NINE FLOORS TO THE ALLEY.

*   *   *

I Would Like To Not Raise Hogs!

(Letter sent to the Secretary of Agriculture)
Dear Mr. Secretary:

My friend Bordereaux received a $1,000 check from the government for *not* raising hogs and so I am going into the *not-raising-hogs* business.

What I want to know is, what is the best kind of land not to raise hogs on and what is the best kind of hogs not to raise? I would prefer not to raise razorbacks, but if this is not the best kind not to raise, I will just as gladly not raise Durocs or Poland Chinas.

The hardest part of this business is going to be keeping an individual record on each of the hogs I do not raise.

My friend Bordereaux has been raising hogs for more than 20 years and the most he ever made was $400 in 1918, until this year when he received $1,000 for not raising hogs. Now, if I get $1,000 for not raising 50 hogs, I will get $2,000 for not raising 100 hogs, etc.

I plan to start off on a small scale, holding myself down to not raising 4,000 hogs for which I will, of course, receive $80,000.

Now these hogs I will not raise will not eat 100,000 bushels of corn. I understand you pay farmers for not raising corn. Will you pay me for not raising 100,000 bushels of corn, which I will not feed to the hogs which I am not raising?

I want to get started as soon as possible, as this looks like a good time of year for not raising hogs.

Yours very truly,
Octover Brussard

*   *   *

The Isms

COMMUNISM: If you have two cows, you give both cows to the government, and then the government sells you some of the milk.

SOCIALISM: If you have two cows, you give both cows to the government, and then the government gives you some of the milk.

NAZIISM: If you have two cows, the government shoots you and takes both cows.

FACISM: If you have two cows, you milk both of them and give the government half of the milk.

NEW DEALISM: If you have two cows, you kill one, milk the other and pour the milk down the drain.

CAPITALISM: If you have two cows, you sell one cow and buy a bull.

*   *   *

PUNISHMENT

"I was a Kamikaze flier during the war," said a Japanese man who was named Chow Mein.

"How could that be? That was a suicide squad."

"Oh, they called me Chicken Chow Mein."

*   *   *

"Do you ever have fights and trouble?" the tourist asked an Indian.

"Oh, no," replied the Indian. "We are just one big Hopi family."

*   *   *

Q. Why did the boy name his rooster Robinson?
A. Because it Crusoe.

*   *   *

Two detectives were standing over a dead man named Juan.

1st detective: He was killed with a golf gun.

2nd detective: What is a golf gun?

1st detective: I don't know, but it sure made a hole in Juan.

*   *   *

"What is the name of your dog?"

"Ginger."

"Does Ginger bite?"

"No, Ginger snaps."

*   *   *

Teacher: When was Rome built?

Student: It was built during the night.

Teacher: The night? Where did you ever get such an idea?

Student: Well, everyone knows that Rome wasn't built in a day.

*   *   *

Q. What did Benedict Arnold's wife say to him at breakfast time?

A. Eggs, Benedict?

105

Joe: Did you hear about the guy that bought two authentic pearl buttons from the South Sea Isle of Bali?

Moe: No, what about him?

Joe: He is the only guy in town with two pearl Bali buttons.

*   *   *

Q. Why did the crow sit on the telephone line?
A. Because he was making a long distance caw.

*   *   *

"My uncle changed his will six times in three years."

"Aha! A fresh heir fiend!"

*   *   *

Ned: I am going to feed my sheep ironized yeast.
Jed: Why are you going to do that?
Ned: So I'll be able to get steel wool.

*   *   *

Mr. & Mrs. Smith were touring Russia. Their guide's name was Rudolph and Mr. Smith and Rudolph argued all the time. As the couple was leaving Moscow, the husband said, "Look, it's snowing out."

The guide disagreed, "No, sir, it's raining out."

"I still think it's snowing," said Mr. Smith.

But his wife replied, "Rudolph the Red knows rain, dear."

*   *   *

Phil: Aren't you rather warm doing your painting all bundled up like that?

Bill: Well, it says right here on the paint can to be sure to put on three coats.

* * *

Max looked up at the steep icy mountainside. "I can't do it." he said.

His companions begged him to climb the mountain with them. But he refused to move. "I'm against mountain climbing," he said.

Now they call him "Anti-climb-Max."

* * *

Ted: Do you know Art?

Fred: Art who?

Ted: Artesian.

Fred: Sure, I know artesian well.

* * *

A housewife in Tibet smelled something burning in the kitchen, rushed in and saw smoke pouring out of the oven. "Oh, my baking yak!" she said.

* * *

Three polar bears were sitting on an iceberg. All were cold and quiet. Finally, the father bear said, "Now I've a tale to tell."

"I, too, have a tale to tell," said the mother bear.

"The little polar bear looked up at his parents and said, "My tale is told!"

* * *

Did you hear about the count that sole the king's crown? They tried and tried to make him confess but he would not. Finally, they said, "We will chop off your head if you don't tell us." He would not tell them so they took him to the chopping block. They told him that he would have one more chance but he did not take it. As the head chopper started down with the ax, the count said, "All right, I'll tell you." It was too late . . . his head went rolling to the ground.

Moral: Don't hatchet your counts before they chicken.

*   *   *

Did you hear about the tribe in Africa that stole the king's throne from a rival tribe? They hid the throne in the rafters of their grass hut. The men who stole the throne were having a party in the hut. They were feeling happy about their successful theft when all of a sudden the rafters broke and the throne fell down and killed all of the men.

Moral: Those who live in grass houses shouldn't stow thrones.

*   *   *

Father: We have a new baby in our house.
Friend: I bet he reigns as king in your family now.
Father: No, Prince of Wails.

*   *   *

Mr. Handy was putting up a knotty pine wall in his living room. His young son came along and said, "What are those holes for?"

"They're knot holes," replied the father.

"Well, then," said the boy, "if they're not holes, what are they?"

Timmy: My grandfather has a wooden leg.
Jimmy: Well, my grandmother has a cedar chest.

*   *   *

"Do you like raisin bread?"
"Don't know, I never tried raisin' any."

*   *   *

"Did you ever hear the rope joke?"
"No."
"Skip it."

*   *   *

Once there was an Indian named Shortcake. When he died, squaw bury Shortcake.

*   *   *

Dick: A snake just snapped at me.
Don: Snakes don't snap, they coil and strike.
Dick: This one was a garter snake.

*   *   *

Girl: Did you hear about the cow that gives buttermilk?
Boy: Buttermilk? That's ridiculous!
Girl: No, it isn't. Have you ever heard of a cow that gives anything but her milk?

*   *   *

John: Are you going to take the car out in weather like this?

Don: Sure! It's a driving rain, isn't it?

* * *

First Roman (at Christian massacre): We've got a capacity crowd, but still we're losing money. The upkeep on the lions must be pretty heavy.

Second Roman: Yes, sir, these lions sure do eat the prophets.

* * *

"I saw a big rat in my cookstove and when I went for my revolver, he ran out."
"Did you shoot him?"
"No. He was out of my range."

* * *

"Give an example of period furniture."
"Well, I should say an electric chair because it ends a sentence."

* * *

Did you hear about the dog who played Bach?
He was about to be auditioned by a TV producer. The dog's agent warned the producer that this was a very sensitive dog, and that "you had better listen to him play, because, if you don't, he loses his temper and leaps at you."
The dog started to play. He was awful. The TV producer patiently waited out the performance. When it was over, he declared angrily, "I should have let him attack. I'm sure his Bach is worse than his bite."

* * *

Did you hear about the fellow that went carp

fishing? As he was about to throw his first cast, his wallet fell out of his pocket into the lake. A carp grabbed the wallet and started to swim away with it. Suddenly, another carp ate the carp that had eaten the wallet. Then, yet another, even larger carp came along and swallowed the carp that ate the carp that devoured the wallet.

And that's how carp-to-carp walleting began.

* * *

An artist decided to buy a new easel. He wasn't too sure what type to get. At the art shop they offered him two, a big one and a small one. He pondered for a while and finally decided on the lesser of two easels.

* * *

"Did you hear about the coed who, when she went to college, found that she wasn't the only pebble on the beach?"

"No, what happened?"

"She became a little bolder."

* * *

Did you hear about the inventor that came up with a knife that would slice two loaves of bread at the same time? He sold it to a large bakery. He then developed a knife that could slice three loaves of bread at the same time? He sold that idea, too!

Finally, the ultimate. He made a huge knife that could cut four loaves of bread at the same time! And so was born the world's first four-loaf cleaver.

* * *

SCHOOL DAZE

"If the Dean of Students doesn't take back what he said to me I am going to leave college."
"What did he say?"
"He told me to leave college."

* * *

Professor: Can you tell me anything about the great philosophers of the 9th century?
Student: They are all dead.

* * *

Son: Dad, do you remember when you told me you got kicked out of college?
Father: Yes, son.
Son: I guess it is true that history repeats itself.

* * *

Teacher: Not only is he the worst behaved child in my class, but he also has a perfect attendance record!

* * *

Professor to students: If you get this information in your brain you will have it in a nutshell.

* * *

Teacher: Who was Joan of Arc?
Student: She must have been Noah's wife.

* * *

Professor: Give me three collective nouns.

Student: Flypaper, wastebasket and vacuum cleaner.

*   *   *

Teacher: If I have ten flies on my back, and I hit one with my book, how many would be left?
Student: The dead one.

*   *   *

Teacher: If I take five apples from ten apples, what's the difference?
Student: That's what I say ... what's the difference?

*   *   *

Professor: Mr. Brown, what do you know about syntax?
Student: Gosh, I didn't know they had to pay tax for their sins.

*   *   *

The teacher wrote the following sentence on the blackboard and asked her pupils to paraphrase it: "He was bent on seeing her."
Little Johnny turned in this paraphrase: "The sight of her doubled him up."

*   *   *

"Johnny, what is a synonym?"
"A synonym is a word you use when you can't spell the other one."

*   *   *

Professor: A fool can ask more questions than a wise old man can answer.

Student: No wonder so many of us flunk our exams.

* * *

Teacher: What happened in 1809?
Student: Lincoln was born.
Teacher: Now, what happened in 1812?
Student: He had his third birthday.

* * *

"I got an underwater mark on that last test."
"What kind of grade is that?"
"Below 'C' level."

* * *

SMOKE SCREEN

Did you hear about the man who read that smoking was bad for your health? He immediately gave up reading.

* * *

She: Would you like to chew my gum, sir?
He: Of course not! It has been in your mouth!
She: And I, sir, would not like to breathe the smoke from your cigarette.

* * *

It's the easiest thing in the world to give up smoking. I know one person who has done it a hundred times.

* * *

The man bought a cigar in a department store and lit it while he was still in the store. A clerk told him to put it out because smoking wasn't allowed in the store.

"What do you mean?" he said. "You sell cigars but don't allow smoking?"

"We also sell bath towels," said the girl sweetly.

* * *

There is a new cigarette with ear plugs in every pack. It's for people who don't want to hear why they should quit smoking.

* * *

Did you ever notice the haze lying over the strip? That isn't smog, it's marijuana fumes.

* * *

I don't smoke but I chew. Don't blow your smoke on me and I won't spit on you.

* * *

"Would you like a cigarette?"
"No, thank you. I think I already have cancer!"

* * *

"Will my smoking this cigar bother you?"
"Not if my getting sick won't bother you!"

*   *   *

Smoking a cigarette won't send you to Hell. It just makes you smell like you've been there.

*   *   *

Did you hear about the man who had a weird accident? He fell asleep smoking in bed, burned a hole in his water bed and drowned.

*   *   *

Sign in service station: NO SMOKING. IF YOUR LIFE ISN'T WORTH ANYTHING, OUR GASOLINE IS!

*   *   *

SPEAKING AND INTRODUCTIONS

After an introduction where the audience stands: "It makes me uneasy for people to stand when I'm introduced at a banquet. I'm always afraid they're going to walk out and leave me to do all the dishes."

*   *   *

Introducing a speaker: There isn't anything that I wouldn't do for Mr. _____, and there isn't anything he wouldn't do for me. That's why we have gone through life not doing anything for each other.

*   *   *

Seated next to a blowhard at a U.N. dinner was an

Oriental fellow dressed in the robes of one of the Far Eastern countries.

The blowhard, attempting to make conversation, leaned over and said: "You like soupee?" The Chinese fellow nodded his head. "You like steakee?" The Oriental nodded again.

As it turned out, the guest speaker at the dinner was our Oriental friend who got up and delivered himself a beautiful fifty-minute address on the U.N. definition of encouragement to self-reliance by under-developed countries of the world. The speech was in flawless Oxford English.

He returned to his place at the head of the table, sat down and turned to his dinner partner and said: "You like speechee?"

*　　*　　*

When he finally finished his speech, there was a great wakening.

*　　*　　*

Speaker: This is terrible! I am the speaker at this banquet and I forget my false teeth!

Man: I happen to have an extra pair, try these.

Speaker: Too small!

Man: Well, try this pair.

Speaker: Too big!

Man: I have one pair left.

Speaker: These fit just fine. It sure is lucky to sit next to a dentist!

Man: I'm not a dentist. I am an undertaker.

*　　*　　*

Only one man applauded; he was slapping his head to keep awake.

* * *

Introduction: Here is a young man who recently appeared at the Policeman's Ball where he sang for the cops. Here's that dirty stool pigeon now.

* * *

I will not make a long, boring speech introducing (speaker's name), he will . . .

* * *

History repeats itself . . . and so does this guy!

* * *

The fault with many speakers is that you can't hear what they're saying. The trouble with him is that you can.

* * *

After applause:
'I feel like a cow on a cold morning. Thank you for that warm hand."
"That one left some of you holding the bag!"
"Well, at least that's better than the utter joke!"

* * *

I was a young fellow when this speech started!

* * *

I will speak only fifteen minutes at most because of my throat. Your chairman threatens to cut it.

* * *

During a long lecture a speaker suffered many interruptions from a man in the balcony who kept yelling: "Louder! Louder!"

After about the fifth interruption, a gentleman in the first row stood up, looked back and asked: "What's the matter, my friend, can't you hear?"

"No, I can't hear," came the answer from the balcony.

"Well, then, be thankful and shut up!"

* * *

"He's such a great speaker, I'd rather hear him speak than eat."

"Me, too. I sat at the head table with him. I've heard him eat."

* * *

"You heard my speech, Professor. Do you think it would improve my delivery if I followed the example of Demosthenes and practiced my diction and elocution with pebbles and marbles in my mouth?"

"I would recommend quick-dry cement."

* * *

The entire audience was hissing him except one man. He was applauding the hissing.

* * *

After an introduction like that, I can hardly wait to hear what I am going to say, myself.

* * *

A lecture is something that can make you feel numb at one end and dumb at the other.

*   *   *

"Did his speech have a happy ending?"
"Sure, everybody was glad it was over."

*   *   *

At a banquet, several long-winded speakers covered almost every subject possible.

When yet another speaker rose, he said, "It seems to me everything has already been talked about. But if someone will tell me what to talk about, I will be grateful."

From the back of the room a voice shouted, "Talk about a minute!"

*   *   *

I am always amazed how an after-dinner speaker can eat chicken and ham and be so full of bull.

*   *   *

Did you hear about the wife of a speaker who took her husband's temperature with a barometer instead of a thermometer. It read Dry and Windy.

*   *   *

In order to become a good speaker you must go to diction school. They teach you how to speak clearly. To do this they fill your mouth with marbles and you're supposed to talk clearly right through the marbles. Now every day you lose one marble. When you've lost all your marbles . . . .

*   *   *

In his last appearance, he drew a line three blocks long. Then they took his chalk away.

*   *   *

I love this place. I've come here for six consecutive years and I look back on them as the best years of my life. Which'll give you some idea of what a miserable life I've been leading!

*   *   *

Our speaker this evening requires no introduction . . . He failed to show up!

*   *   *

Introduction: Next, we have a young man who's done so much in so little time, it's kinda hard to exaggerate his accomplishments . . . but I'll do my best.

*   *   *

Ladies and gentlemen, . . . I guess that takes in most of you.

*   *   *

He's always offering "sound advice" . . . 99% sound and 1% advice.

*   *   *

He's suffering from I-strain.

*   *   *

He's an M.C. all right . . . a mental case.

*   *   *

He speaks straight from the shoulder. Too bad his remarks don't start from higher up.

*   *   *

Did you hear about the man who was speaking and someone in the audience went to sleep during his boring talk. He got so mad that he took the gavel and hit the sleeping man in the head. The sleeper woke up, took a long look at the speaker and said, "Hit me again. I can still hear you."

*   *   *

An introduction like this is like flattery. And flattery is like perfume . . . it is to be sniffed but not swallowed.

*   *   *

You have heard it said before that this speaker needs no introduction. Well, I have heard him and he needs all the introduction he can get.

*   *   *

Every time he opens his mouth, he puts his feats in.

*   *   *

Year ago he was an unknown failure . . . now he's a known failure.

*   *   *

He's an expert at handing out baloney disguised as food for thought.

* * *

He reminds you of a bee . . . a humbug.

* * *

He talks in stereophonic style . . . out of both sides of his mouth.

* * *

He's a real drip. You can always hear him but can rarely turn him off.

* * *

He reminds you of a clarinet . . . a wind instrument.

* * *

Our speaker has not only all of the five senses but he has two more, horse and common.

* * *

He could talk his head off and never miss it.

* * *

His mouth is so big, he can whisper in his own ear.

* * *

What he needs is a little lockjaw.

* * *

We have a strange and wonderful relationship. He's strange and I'm wonderful.

* * *

Nervous? If the butterflies in my stomach ever got together, they could carry me right outta here.

* * *

He needs no introduction. What he needs is a conclusion.

* * *

He's the type who approaches every subject with an open mouth.

* * *

He wearies you with the patter of little feats.

* * *

He never opens his mouth unless he has nothing to say.

* * *

He can wrap up a one-minute idea in a one-hour vocabulary.

* * *

He has a diarrhea of words and a constipation of ideas.

* * *

His most interesting point is the point of departure.

* * *

He's an I-specialist.

* * *

His I's are too close together.

* * *

And now in response to numerous requests ... Goodnight, folks!

* * *

An inexperienced speaker arose in confusion after dinner and murmured stumblingly:

"M-m-my f-f-friends, when I came here tonight, only God and myself knew what I was about to say to you ... and now only God knows."

* * *

"His last speech had the audience in the aisles."
"Applauding?"
"No, stretching and yawning."

* * *

If he said what he thought, he'd be speechless.

* * *

Speaker: Did you notice how my voice filled the town hall?

Man: Yes, in fact, I noticed several people leave to make room for it.

*　　*　　*

After a long-winded introduction: The very kind observations of the chairman remind me of the man who was attending a formal banquet. He put a large forkful of steaming, hot baked potato into his mouth, which he instantly spat out upon his plate. Looking about at his disconcerted fellow guests and at his hostess, he remarked blandly, "Only an idiot would have swallowed that."

*　　*　　*

You have been giving your attention to a turkey stuffed with sage; you are now about to consider a sage stuffed with turkey.

*　　*　　*

They call him the "Mastoid of Ceremonies" . . . he's a pain in the ear.

*　　*　　*

His wisecracks are always greeted with a tremendous burst of silence.

*　　*　　*

Every year he takes a boast-to-boast tour.

*　　*　　*

Just encourage him and you'll be slain by the jawbone of an ass.

*　　*　　*

He holds people open-mouthed with his conversations. They can't stop yawning.

* * *

I have been told that the mind cannot absorb any more than the seat can endure.

* * *

Introduced for a full half hour by a local big shot who fancied himself as an orator, a lecturer assured his audience, "Now I know how a pancake must feel after too much syrup has been poured over it." Another speaker, under similar circumstances, began, "After the whirlwind, the still, small voice . . . "

* * *

His ideas are sound . . . all sound.

* * *

He was such a bad speaker the audience hissed the ushers.

* * *

I have the microphone and there is the loud speaker!

* * *

M.C.: (introducing speaker:) You have only to put a dinner in his mouth and out comes a speech.
Speaker: Our M.C. is also unusual. You have only to put a speech into his mouth and out comes your dinner.

* * *

The other day I was in Los Angeles and heard a disk jockey on the radio named Heck (*last name of person you are introducing*). Are you related to him? They will always answer, "No!" To which you reply, "That's strange! You sure look like Heck to me!"

*   *   *

I would like to present the funniest, most talented, most outstanding speaker and the fellow who wrote this introduction for me . . . .

*   *   *

And now I'm going to say something in the public interest . . Goodnight.

*   *   *

I spoke to a group of hippies and they're a tough audience. They don't laugh or applaud . . . they're too busy scratching!

*   *   *

Sign on speaker's table: "If you don't strike oil in twenty minutes, stop boring."

*   *   *

Quiet please. Quiet please. Let's come to order. It's time for the speaker. You can enjoy yourselves some other time.

*   *   *

Every time I stand up to speak my mind sits down!

*   *   *

That was the sort of speech that gives failure a bad name.

*   *   *

In Biblical days, it was considered a miracle when a donkey spoke. Listening to him, you can't help but realize how times have changed.

*   *   *

After a dinner program like this, a speaker is like parsley . . . not really needed.

*   *   *

Chauncey Depew once played a trick upon Mark Twain on an occasion when they were both to speak at a banquet. Twain spoke first for some 20 minutes and was received with great enthusiasm. When Depew's turn came immediately afterwards, he said, "Mr. Toastmaster, Ladies and Gentlemen, before this dinner, Mark Twain and I made an agreement to trade speeches. He has just delivered mine and I'm grateful for the reception you have accorded it. I regret that I have lost his speech and cannot remember a thing he had to say."

He sat down with much applause.

*   *   *

THAT'S SPORTING

"I can't see why you play golf with him. He's a bad loser."

"I'd rather play with a bad loser than a winner any time."

* * *

It was hunting season when a state trooper walked up to a man and his son, and said, "That's a nice buck you have on the top of your car." The surprised man couldn't say anything, so his son answered for him, "That's nothing! You should see the one we have in the trunk!"

* * *

Boxer: Have I done any damage?
Trainer: No, but keep swinging. The draft might give him a cold.

* * *

There are two kinds of hunters ... Those who hunt for sport and those who catch something.

* * *

Golfer: "Pardon me, but would you mind if I played through? I've just heard that my wife has been taken seriously ill."

"When I was in India," said the club bore, "I saw a tiger come down to the water where some women were washing clothes. It was a very fierce tiger, but one woman, with great presence of mind, splashed some water in its face and it slunk away."

"Gentlemen," said a man in an armchair, "I can vouch for the truth of this story. Some minutes after this incident, I was coming down to the water. I met this tiger, and, as is my habit, stroked its whiskers. Gentlemen, those whiskers were wet."

*   *   *

Two boxers had placed bets and each backed himself to lose the fight. During the progress of the bout, one accidently hit his opponent a light tap on the face. He immediately laid down and the referee proceeded to count him out. The other boxer was in a quandary. Just as the referee got to nine, he had a magnificent idea come to him. He rushed to the prostrate man and kicked him, and was instantly disqualified.

*   *   *

Two hunters had been out several hours and one of them had been growing uneasy. Finally panic overtook him. "We're lost!" he cried to his companion. "What shall we do?"

"Keep your shirt on!" said his companion. "Shoot an extra deer and the game warden will be here in a minute and a half."

*   *   *

Sportsman: Is there much good hunting in these parts?

Native: Sure, there's plenty of hunting but very little finding.

*   *   *

Talkative hunter: Once while I was having a meal in the jungle, a lion came so close to me that I could feel his breath on the back of my neck. What did I do?

Bored listener: Turned your collar up?

* * *